IN-HOUSE TEAM

Editor: Mike Toller

Features editor: Alexi Duggins

Senior editorial assistant: Joly Braime

Editorial and production assistant: Alix F...

Editorial assistance: Anton Tweedale, C... Gardiner, Kelsey Strand-Polyak, Katy Georgiou

Designer: Sarah Winter

Design assistance: Caitlin Kenney, Sara Gramner

Picture research: Alex Amend

Production consultant: Iain Leslie

Web editor: Cameron J Macphail

National ad sales: Sue Ostler, Zee Ahmad

Local ad sales: Gemma Coldwell

Distribution: Nativeps

Financial controller: Sharon Evans

Managing director: Ian Merricks

Publisher: Itchy Group

© 2007 Itchy Group

ISBN: 978-1-905705-22-1

Photography: Rebecca Lee, Joe Millson, Mike Laing, Antony O'Hanlon, Dorrottya Verses, Chris Grossmeier, Bas Driessen, Selma Yalazi Dawani, Mario Alberto, Tim Ireland

Illustrations: Tom Denbigh, Si Clark, Joly Braime

Cover illustration: Si Clark (www.si-clark.co.uk)

Itchy Group
White Horse Yard
78 Liverpool Road
London, N1 0QD
Tel: 020 7288 9810
Fax: 020 7288 9815
E-mail: editor@itchymedia.co.uk
Web: www.itchycity.co.uk

No part of this publication may be copied or reproduced, stored in any retrieval system or transmitted in any form without the prior permission of the publishers. The publishers cannot accept any responsibility for inaccuracies, or for changes made since publication, or for any other loss – direct or inconsequential – arising in connection with the information in this publication. Acceptance of advertisements does not imply recommendation by the publisher.

The views expressed in this publication are not necessarily those held by the editors or publishers. Readers are advised to form their own opinions and we welcome any further contributions. All details, listings, prices, addresses and phone numbers are correct to our knowledge at the time of going to press. Itchy cannot be held responsible for any breach of copyright arising from the supply of artwork from advertisers.

www.itchymanchester.co.uk

olivier *morosini*
HAIRDRESSING

Mon–Wed, 9am–6pm; Thu, 10am–8pm;
Fri, 9.30am–6pm; Sat, 9am–4pm
98 Tib Street, Northern Quarter, Manchester, M4 1LR
T: (0161) 832 8989
MORE INFORMATION AT WWW.ITCHYMANCHESTER.CO.UK

Welcome to Itchy 2007

You lucky thing, you. Whether you've bought, borrowed, begged or pinched it off your best mate's bookshelf, you've managed to get your mucky paddles on an Itchy guide. And what a guide it is. If you're a regular reader, you're probably already impressing your friends with your dazzling knowledge of where to head for a rip-roaring time. If, on the other hand, you're a trembling Itchy virgin, then get ready to live life as you've never lived it before. We've spent the last year scouring Manchester for the very best places to booze, cruise, schmooze, snooze and lose ourselves to the forces of pleasure. As ever, we've made the necessary, erm, sacrifices in the name of our research – dancing nights away, shopping 'til we flop and of course, eating and drinking more than we ever thought possible. But we're still alive, and now we're ready to do the whole lot again. Come with us if you're up for it – the first round's on us...

KEY TO SYMBOLS
- **◐** Opening times
- **🍴** Itchy's favourite dish
- **∅** Cost of a bottle of house wine
- **£** Admission price

Introduction — 5
Welcome to Manchester, welcome to Itchy. Here's the lowdown on all the high life

Eat — 9
Hungry? We know where you can fill your boots and bellies

Drink — 29
There's nothing like going for a drink or 12. Wet your whistles in these pubs and bars

Dance — 55
From hot-steppers to headbangers, we've got good news for anyone who wants to shake it

Gay — 65
See and be seen on the scene, whichever way you swing

Shop — 71
We'll help you find that shoe/shirt/rare seven-inch you've been looking for

Out & about — 87
Live music, comedy, museums, theatres and galleries. What are you waiting for?

Laters — 103
Late-night living for night owls and 24-hour party people

Sleep — 109
Voulez-vous coucher avec nous ce soir? Our pick of bargain beds and fancy four-posters

Useful info — 115
Everything else you need to survive, from beauty salons to balti houses

Map & index — 122
Lost again? Better get busy with Itchy's handy map and index then...

www.itchymanchester.co.uk

...AND ON THE SIXTH DAY, GOD CREATED MANCHESTER

Introduction

Welcome to Manchester

'On the sixth day, God created Manchester.'
Probably not Richard Dawkins.

The BFG of Great Britain, Manchester is a metropolis with heart. We've got heart. We've got soul. We've got Müller yoghurts. A melting pot of entertainment, culture and obscure monuments, Manchester has rightly earned its (unofficial) title as 'The Best City to Go to Ever in the History of Known Civilisation: 2007'.

We've got massive monuments, we've got sprawling shopping centres, we've got pigeons. But unlike certain soulless capitals of the South, we've also got sass. Sass and spunk. Sass and spunk and style. From the obscure poems that adorn the pubs in Rusholme to the potential human kebab that is the B of the Bang statue, this is a city full of soul. Seriously. Lionel Richie comes here for inspiration. Just listen to the chorus of *All Night Long* – 'Were going to/party/Fallowfield/Canal Street/forever.' At least we think that's what he's singing.

And like the brave advocates of Slim Fast that we are (seriously, try a White Russian with Slim Fast in, you fall over and you lose weight at the same time), we've stepped up to the plate and tried to squeeze it all into an A5 guide book. But lo, far from being the literary version of a double-decker bus tour, this guide is your insider trader for everything Manchester has to offer. We've explored, foraged and got punched a couple of times – all to bring you the most comprehensive guide to this fair city. And unlike a bus tour, you won't have to put up with the incessant clicking of camera shutters and feverish murmurs every time you pass a sign pointing to Old Trafford. We know this city inside and out, and just like a Jedi knight, we're passing our knowledge right on to you. Just don't use it for evil and start killing other Jedis. It's frowned upon, and frankly it's going to hurt our book sales, so don't do it.

Pack your Elmo rucksack with supplies (but don't forget folks – no cigarettes unless you want to end up being bounced upside down on the pavement by some smoke-hating fascist), grab your walking stick and hit the streets. With your trusty Itchy guide in hand, venture out into the morning sunlight and take full advantage of this fabulous, sexy, quirky, fantastic, (various other adjectives) city. You won't regret it.

Introduction

Two hours in Manchester

While Jack Bauer can scoot across Los Angeles in the same commercial break that barely gave us time to get to the john, those of us without a super-fast secret service escort (hell, not even a Ford Escort) should stick to the city centre.

If you're hankering for a spot of shopping, head to Market Street and the fantabulous Triangle Centre. If you've got a few minutes spare, you can wander up to Deansgate, peer into the expensive shops and wish you could afford a £500 handbag. You probably can't, so it's best if you don't even think about it.

If you're a spot peckish after all that, grab a traditional pub lunch at The Shakespeare (16 Fountain Street, 0161 834 5515). A country pub plonked in the middle of the city, its dinners are mega tasty and infinitely better than a £5 train chicken sarnie.

With your digital stopwatch about to beep, nip to Chinatown and the celebrity-esque Canal Street. Both are Manchester landmarks and are almost necessary sights in a whistle stop tour of the city.

Congratulations, you've just spent two hours running around Manchester. You should feel proud, cultured and about 20 stone lighter.

Introduction

Two days in Manchester

SHUT EYE – Those of you wanting to spend your pennies on better things like beer and sambucca should hit the Ibis (96 Portland Street, 0161 272 5000), a comfy hotel where you can snooze for a mere fifty-five pounds. Other safe bets include the Britannia Hotel (35 Portland Street, 0161 236 9154) and The Castlefield Hotel (Liverpool Road, 0161 832 7073).

CHOW – Particularly fussy palates need to pass through Wagamama (1a The Printworks, 0161 839 5916) or Croma (1 Clarence Street, 0161 237 9799). Offering Oriental and Italian menus respectively, both are classy restaurants without the heart-stopping prices. If you enjoy spending your entire bank balance on a hearty meal, then we'd advise you pay a visit to Le Mont (Level 5 and 6, Urbis, Cathedral Gardens, 0161 605 8282) or Panacea (14 John Dalton Street, 0161 833 0000). Both are award-winning, wallet-robbing restaurants.

'TIL YOU DROP – Market Street is the hub of Manchester's shopping district and you'll find your usual high street suspects down here. The plethora of clothes and music stores around the Northern Quarter offer up some unique and inexpensive gear, whilst St Ann's Square is home to the catwalk brands.

GLUG – The Cornerhouse (70 Oxford Street, 0161 200 1508) is always good for a couple of bevvies – it's home to the artistic and creative inhabitants of Manchester, so expect a cracking atmosphere. While you're around this part of town, Fab Café (111 Portland Street, 0161 236 2019) and Kro (325 Oxford Road, 0161 274 3100) are both worth a look. If you're after more stylish bars, the Northern Quarter can happily accommodate your whims, although Odd (30–32 Thomas Street, 0161 833 0070) is by far the trump card in this pack.

DANCE – Cheese lovers should go directly to Bar 38 (Peter Street, 0161 835 3076) and Brannigan's (Peter Street, 0161 835 9697). Indie kids need to hit 42nd Street (2 Bootle Street, 0161 831 7108) or 5th Avenue (121 Princess Streeet, 0161 236 2754). Both have loud music to shout along to. The Music Box (65a Oxford Road, 0161 273 5200) and Sankey's (Radium Street, 0161 950 4201) cater for the glo-stick collective, and their nights are always something special.

ATTRACTIONS – No trip to Manchester is complete without a bit of sightseeing. Culture Casanovas need directions to the museum, art gallery and the glass mammoth of Urbis. Music pilgrims should check out Night and Day Café (26 Oldham Street, 0161 236 4597) – new music is born here, wailing and surrounded by drunk midwives.

www.itchymanchester.co.uk

OPEN 7 DAYS A WEEK
12.00pm to 12.00am
87–91 Wilmslow Road, Rusholme,
Manchester M14 5SU
Tel: (0161) 257 0006

THE BEST CURRY IN MANCHESTER

20% off every meal
with the Al Bilal Student Loyalty Card

"Al Bilal is my favourite curry restaurant"
Dr. Chris Steele
ITV's *This Morning*

Collect Loyalty Card Stamps to get your 6th MEAL FREE!

Air conditioned restaurant

TRY OUR LOW FAT DIET

Eat

Eat

CAFÉS

Café Muse
Manchester Museum, Oxford Road
(0161) 275 3220

After a hard day of avoiding screaming kids at the Manchester Museum and scowling at drunken students on the nearby campus, you'd be forgiven for wanting a quiet sit down and a coffee. Thankfully, the intellectual refuge of Café Muse can happily replenish the most tired and restless of souls. Or maybe that's just the caffeine. We've yet to decide. A relaxing environment that you don't have to eat mushrooms for, this is worth popping into if you're sick to death of your soya milk, double-shot, venti latte with sprinkles.

Mon-Sun, 8.30am-6pm

Gemini Café
328 Oxford Road
(0161) 273 8839

Itchy has jumped on the award ceremony bandwagon. We've seen the Baftas, the Oscars and the Primark Awards for the Best-Dressed Scally and we want in. We want an excuse to wear tuxedos. We want a red carpet with flashing bulbs. We want Stephen Fry to say witty things on stage. If this dream ever became reality, then Gemini would win the 'Best Hangover Cure in Manchester'. Granted, they serve their eggs and sausages with a healthy side order of grease, but as most of the clientele are either off their tits or wearing dark glasses (or both), we don't think anyone minds.

Mon-Sat, 9am-8pm; Sun, 11am-5pm

Café Pop
34-36 Oldham Street
(0161) 236 5797

Deep in the bowels of this retro Oldham Street shop, you'll find a cosy little nook for a quiet coffee and a chat. It's a bit like walking into a 1970s car boot sale, meaning that while you sip your beverage of choice, you can ponder who thought it would be a good idea to mass-produce so much tacky crap. Strangely enough though, it all works. Lava lamps happily sit next to 1960s footwear and you feel strangely nostalgic for the good old days. At least until you realise they didn't have the internet or any other of these newfangled mod cons, that is.

Mon-Sat, 10.30am-5.30pm;
Sun, 11am-4.30pm

The Koffee Pot
21 Hilton Street
(07970) 101 699

Time was, the Koffee Pot was a scary place to be in. A haunt for the local construction population, you'd need to be attired in a luminous jacket and a hardhat to get through the door. Blessed be the influence of the nearby Oldham Street then, as the Koffee Pot, now Northern Quartered-up, has been transformed into a place of happiness and kittens. Walls of funky graffiti, a flat screen television playing *Only Fools and Horses* and coffee that would satisfy the most caffeine deprived yuppie mean that this is now a place you can happily be seen in without the need to dig around in your costume box for that *Bob the Builder* hat.

Mon-Sun, 7am-4pm

Eat

Oklahoma
74–76 High Street
(0161) 834 1136

Bright, cheerful, and deliciously tacky, this should be the first landmark on your coffee drinking adventure through the Northern Quarter. Whilst we're not entirely sure what the shop sells, and are quietly convinced that it defies all genres of any category, the coffee shop is a delightful little place where you can while away the hours and pretend you're not in Manchester anymore. So, sit back with your large latte and hum a few bars of *Over the Rainbow* as the rain streams down the windows. That is, until you remember that Dorothy came from Kansas and that joke is totally redundant. Fairly ye be warned.

Mon–Sat, 8am–7pm; Sun, 11am–5pm

Olive Delicatessen
Regency House, 36–38 Whitworth Street
(0161) 236 2360

Not to fall in love with Olive would be virgin on the ridiculous. Putting the 'pant' in 'pantry', this place does things so sensuous to your tongue that they're practically illegal. Think spiced, pop-your-cherry chutneys on panini melts with earthy hummous, gourmet coffee with enough caffeinated magic to wake the dead, and gâteaux-fabulous cakes and breads. There's even a loaf called an 'Orlando'; is it a Bloom-er, Itchy wonders? Their colossal spirits selection includes the most potent vodka in the world. Our recommendation to visit is no less strong.

Mon–Fri, 8am–10pm;
Sat–Sun, 9am–10pm

The Titchy Coffee Company
The Triangle, Exchange Square
(0161) 835 1540

Top fifteen things that team Itchy likes to put in our mouths (what? Don't tell us you don't have one of these lists yourself): 1. Old pen lids. 2. Bread sticks. 3. The amazing smoothies from The Titchy Coffee Company. 4. Television remotes. 5. Cigarettes. 6. Rival guides to Manchester. 7. Deodorant cans. 8. Alcohol we haven't bought for ourselves. 9. Alcohol in general. 10. Bananas. 11. Rubber bands. 12. Dry spaghetti sticks. 13. Colgate toothpaste. 14. Gum. 15. Chicken sandwiches with lettuce and cucumber and tomato and mayonnaise and Thai sweet chilli crisps.

Mon–Wed, 10am–6pm; Thu–Sat, 10am–7pm; Sun, 11am–5pm

www.itchymanchester.co.uk

Eat

Eighth Day

111 Oxford Road
(0161) 273 1850

It might make aging blokes sound tastier, but describing a blatantly grey burger as a 'silver fox' doesn't help. 'Salt 'n' pepper' ain't gonna work either – no seasoning can make such weeping gristle appetising. Swap depressing over-processed offcuts for something fresh at Eighth Day. With a changing daily range of veggie and vegan meals and snacks to eat in or take out, it's whole-some and delicious-everything. They're licensed to serve alcohol, publish their own cookbooks, and do big, boingy, moist birthday cakes to order. Gr-eight.

Mon–Sat, 9.30am–7.30pm
Sat–Sun, 9am–10pm
Bake of the day, £4.80

Eighth Day

Vegetarian Café

Fresh, healthy, vegetarian and vegan food, from a burger to a banquet. All lovingly made by our own cooks.

Health food shop

Huge variety of vegetarian food. Free professional health advice, vitamins and supplements.

Phone Café:	0161 273 1850
Phone Shop:	0161 273 4878
Fax:	0161 273 4869

111 Oxford Road, Manchester, M1 7DU

www.eighth-day.co.uk

On the Eighth Day Co-operative Limited - a Workers' Co-operative. Est. 1970

Eat

RESTAURANTS

Al Bilal
87-91 Wilmslow Road
(0161) 257 0006

As Einstein noted, everything is relative. A mile is a pleasant stroll when you're not in a curry hurry. But choose a bad restaurant and that same curry mile seems tortuously long, as you Rusholme to run an urgent task with little charm, but a whole lot of Charmin. Don't risk it; pick Al Bilal. A two floor paradise established over a decade ago, it's an Itchy favourite for great service and food for little cash and no dash, guaranteed.

Mon–Thu & Sun, 12pm–12am;
Fri–Sat, 12pm–1am
Chicken jalfrezi, £5.90
£12.50

Beluga
2 Mount Street
(0161) 833 3339

A wise prophet once said, 'The Inland Revenue are bad people who will get their comeuppance and their building will be transformed into a lovely restaurant'. Amazingly, this three hundred year old prophecy has come true and Beluga stands as testament to the powers of the crystal ball. Like a religious exorcism, all the bad that this building once held has been wiped clean and replaced by a fantastically urbanite restaurant with not a tax collector in sight. Unless they're eating on the table behind you. Seriously, they're everywhere.

Mon–Thu, 11am–10pm; Fri–Sat,
11am–11pm; Bar, Thu–Sat 11am–2am;
Pan-fried sea bass, £13.95

Eat

Bluu
Unit 1, Thomas Street
(0161) 839 7995

Exceedingly fine, classy-buzzy dining that's also perfectly relaxed, and at three courses for under £20 with the prix fixe menu, it won't give your wallet the Bluus. The basement bar couldn't be cosier if it was lined with fleece and hot water bottles, and angelic staff are particularly good with large parties, ensuring the synchronised arrival of everyone's food. Great for dates, too, if you ever mange to pull someone more decent than the usual beer-goggle ogled wonky donkey Eeyore-phwoar.

Food, Mon–Sun, 12pm–2.30pm & 6pm–10pm; Fri–Sat, 12pm–2.30pm & 6pm–10.30pm
Chicken with brioche dumplings, £13.50
£12.50

Bouzouki by Night
88 Princess Street
(0161) 236 9282

Restaurants and nightclubs are an unusual mix. It's not often you finish off a three course meal and then decide you want to work it off by dancing to the latest happy hardcore remix. For those of you who want to see what it's like to boogie with a bloated stomach, you can't go much wrong with Bouzouki by Night. The food proves our Grecian cousins sure know how to cook. The nearby dance floor proves that they know how to party afterwards. The hangover proves that you drink too much.

Mon–Thu, 5.30pm–1.30am; Fri–Sat, 8pm–3am
Greek banquet, £19.90 per person
£12.50

Café Istanbul
79 Bridge Street
(0161) 833 9942

It's always an awkward moment, poring over the menu, 'umming' and 'erring' on what to have for dinner. With the £5.50-an-hour waiter impatiently tapping pen on pad, it takes a person of Bauer-like sensibilities not to be intimidated. Thankfully, Café Istanbul don't want to see bad CTU agent impressions, and provide a range of set menus for the indecisive among us. A classy Turkish restaurant, its high quality food is noteworthy, as is the friendliness of the staff. We can only surmise they're getting paid over minimum wage. Or have been sniffing the floor cleaner.

Mon–Thu, 12pm–11pm; Fri–Sat, 12pm–11.30pm; Sun, 5.30pm–10pm
Minced lamb meatballs, £3.90

Eat

Casa Tapas
704 Wilmslow Road, Didsbury
(0161) 448 2515

You can't have a bad time under the watchful eye of fairy lights. While these little angels of light bring happiness and joy to most major holidays and occasionally mildew-ridden university accommodation, it's in Casa Tapas where you realise the full extent of their influence. Littering the restaurant, these little guys make your dining experience that little bit more informal. Gone is the quiet muttering from separate tables – this is a full-blown party atmosphere. Yes, this could be because of the nice food, but we're not going to detract from the magical power of fairy lights.

- *Mon–Sat, 11am–11pm*
- *Ribs, £3.40*

Darbar
65 Wilmslow Road
(0161) 224 4392

Meaning 'King's Court', you're unlikely to see Prince Philip here. Just as well, as we'd be subjected to banter about the decline of the British Empire. If we wanted that, we could just talk to our grandparents. Darbar is bright and colourful; a cheery place and well worth a visit if you've got a hankering for a curry, a naan or delusions of grandeur. You'll probably bump ino Prince Charles then.

- *Mon–Thu, 3pm–3am; Fri–Sat, 3pm–4am; Sun, 2pm–2am*
- *King prawn balti, £7.90*

Croma
1 Clarence Street, Off Albert Square
(0161) 237 9799

If you're thumbing through this book in the hope of finding a shiny ten pound note, think again (we already checked). If you're flicking through in the hope of finding a restaurant to take a first date, then your long and tedious search is over. Welcome to Croma. The food's nice, the atmosphere is bubbly and the wine is cheap enough to ensure that you'll find even the most excruciating of first dates brightens up in no time. Or at least you can blame anything really stupid you say (or worse, do) on getting smashed on the house white.

- *Mon–Sat, 12pm–11pm; Sun, 12pm–10.30pm*
- *Fish lasagne, £6.95*
- *£10.95*

The Didsbury Village Restaurant
846 Wilmslow Road, Didsbury
(0161) 445 2552

'Dear DVR, we can't continue with this façade any longer. We can't be with you anymore. We feel our love has become a lie. Maybe if you'd removed half of the tables to allow some privacy, or left the customers alone we wouldn't be having this discussion, but alas, t'was not to be. Au revoir... and can you return our DVDs?'.

- *Mon–Thu, 5.30pm–10pm; Fri–Sat, 5.30pm–10.30pm; Sun, 12pm–9.30pm*
- *Trio of Yorkshire beef, £14.95*
- *£11.95*

 Get there with system one travelcards.co.uk

www.itchymanchester.co.uk

Eat

Dimitri's Taverna

1 Campfield Arcade, Tonman Street
(0161) 839 3319

Nice Dimitri's, Dimitri's, nice. You might even say it's a-meze-ing. If working for a boss with the mental capacity of a semi-conscious turnip has left you more disillusioned than hours of fruitless staring at a magic eye poster, then get your Meds, Greek style, with the restorative quick lunch – the lamb and roast veg sarnie could make us feel good even after being trapped in a confined space for an extended period with David Blaine. So just imagine what the live music and late bar at the weekends could achieve. Now that's what we call magic.

- *Mon–Sun, 11am–12am*
- *Pork souvlakia, £12.55*
- *Retsina, £7.95*

Est Est Est

756 Wilmslow Road, Didsbury
(0161) 445 8209

There is nothing quite as wonderful as outdoor dining: sitting in the sun eating from a light and delicate Italian menu cooked with fresh, seasonal produce and some excellent wine, which is made all the better when there are pretty folk serving your lunch. So it really is kind of a shame about the stonking great B-road spewing its foul sputum over your excellent lunch. A Mediterranean village this ain't. Stick to the indoors in autumn, and don't forget that bus fumes in your lunch are never cool.

- *Mon–Sun, 11am–11pm*
- *Le insalate: spinach, asparagus, pancetta and capers, £8.95*
- *£11.50*

Eat

Evuna
277–279 Deansgate
(0161) 819 2752

With a selection of over 600 Spanish wines, it's probably not a good idea to host a children's party here. Drunken 7-year-olds aren't as much fun as you'd expect. However, if you're after stylish Spanish eating, then you're in luck. The platters are a must and you'd be forgiven for booking an easyJet flight south as soon as you get back home. The fantastic wines that adorn the shelves are also for sale, although we wouldn't recommend sampling them all in one night, because you'll look like a twit when you try and walk.

- *Mon-Sat, 11am-11pm*
- *Chicken skewers, £4.50*
- *£15*

Felicini
60 Oxford Street
(0161) 228 6633

Our favourite Didsbury Italian almost makes the 50p bus trip up to Oxford Road a pleasure in itself. As you'd expect, it's a classy affair – the food is good looking, the staff are delicious and the price isn't going to make you wish you'd plumped for a table for two in Burger King. Which you should never do if you want to remain friends with your dinner buddy. The oblongy-box nature of the restaurant is a tad off-putting, but that's about the only gripe we've got. If Felicini were a girl, she'd be the bella the ball.

- *Mon-Sat, 12pm-11pm; Sun, 11am-11pm*
- *Calzone, £8.50*
- *£12.50*

Fried and tested

The sun is shining through your window. The birds are singing. The milkman is whistling. You couldn't give a shit. You're hung over and you're hungry. To make matters worse, the Shreddies are stale and the milk smells a bit funny. Time to head outdoors (shudder). All of the **Kros** (there are two on Oxford Road) around Manchester offer a great breakfast deal for those of you unfortunate enough to be up in the AM, while the brekkies in **Trof** (2a Landcross Road) are renowned for being the best the mighty Fallowfield has to offer. It's a cosy, converted semi just off Wilmslow road, and perfect for those of you too lazy to make the trip to the nearby Sainsbury's. Stayed over in Didsbury and forgotten which bus to catch? Nip into **Jem & I** (1c School Lane), grab some grub and figure out in which direction the air smells like home.

www.itchymanchester.co.uk

Eat

French Restaurant
Midland Hotel, Peter Street
(0161) 236 3333

While it may not be winning many awards for the most originally-named restaurant, the French Restaurant, embedded deep within the classy Midland hotel, is a joy in Gallic cuisine. As you'd expect from the Midland, the restaurant is a lavish affair. Soft lighting, silver cutlery and pristine white tablecloths mean that a bite here costs a pretty French euro. That said, it's worth every converted penny. The food is top notch, so you can't help but feel disappointed they didn't put as much effort into thinking of the name.
- *Mon–Thu, 7pm–10.30pm; Fri–Sat, 7pm–11pm*
- *Pan fried rib-eye steak, £17.75*
- *£11*

The Greenhouse
331 Great Western Street, Rusholme
(0161) 224 0730

Not a half-dead tomato plant in sign, The Greenhouse is a vegetarian paradise in the middle of curry-orientated Rusholme. Its grass coloured exterior hides some of the best veggie grub this side of a field, and you'd be a chicken-munching clown if you were around the area and didn't pop in to say 'hello'. You'd even get a 'hello' back. After the exchange of greetings, sit down, order some salad and tuck in. Though don't comment on how you could grow better cucumbers in your greenhouse. It's just not polite.
- *Mon–Sat, 6.30am–10pm; Sun, 12pm–3pm*
- *Mexican mixed bean chilli, £6.25*
- *£12*

Gaucho Grill
2a St Mary's Street
(0161) 833 4333

There is no finer feeling than sitting down and eating a cow. Naturally, it has to be cooked right, and an entire meal can be ruined if it just sits there mooing on your plate. Thankfully, the Gaucho Grill knows how to cook steaks. An Argentinian experience that doesn't end in missed penalties, this restaurant is the most stylish way to keep the local cattle population from spiralling out of control. Classy décor and a smiling collection of staff keep you from feeling too guilty about this.
- *Mon–Thu, 12pm–10.30pm; Fri–Sat, 12pm–11pm; Sun, 12pm–10.30pm*
- *Rib-eye steak, £17*
- *£28.50*

Eat

The Grill on the Alley
5 Ridgefield
(0161) 833 3465

Jeremy the lobster was enjoying his day. Staring out of his tank, he began to think what a lucky lobster he was. He had been living in the tank at The Grill on the Alley for a few weeks now and was settling in nicely. Just then, a face appeared at his glass window. 'Hello,' said Jeremy, cheerfully, for he was quite fond of visitors. The person behind the glass pointed straight at Jeremy, which he thought quite rude. Perturbed, he turned his back on the face and began to walk away. He was just thinking what else he could do with his day, when he was suddenly picked up, boiled to death and eaten.

- *Mon–Sun, 12pm–12am*
- *Steak sandwich, £8.50*

Koreana
40a King Street West
(0161) 832 4330

This restaurant specialises in Korean food. We think you should all know this lest you turn up here and ask for fish and chips. No-one wants you to look stupid. If you're a dedicated aficionado of all things McDonald's, fear not, as the helpful staff will gladly walk you through the menu. Those with overly large stomachs might want to invest in the banquet meals – you get a nice pick and mix. Like Woolworths, but more fun. And without lots of small children screaming for Action Men.

- *Mon–Thu, 12pm–2.30pm & 6.30pm–10.30pm; Fri, 12pm–2.30pm & 6.30pm–11pm; Sat, 5.30pm–11pm*
- *Banquet, £18.90*

Grinch
5–7 Chapel Walks
(0161) 907 3210

Down Chapel Walks way Grinch stood, night and day. 'Twas one of the happiest, cheeriest places, where Manc people ate with big smiles on their faces. Sweetly elated, their food they digested. The service was good, no-one contested. Work stress was forgotten, and family, and home; people sat down and and at once ceased to moan. Moan they did not, nor argue no more; for Grinch did make sure that a good time they saw. The décor was nice, bright and sweet. The selection of cocktails went down a treat. But the rhymes were shit.

- *Mon–Sat, 12pm–11pm; Sun, 12pm–10.30pm*
- *Margherita pizza, £5.25*
- *£8.95*

www.itchymanchester.co.uk

Eat

Kro Bar
325 Oxford Road
(0161) 274 3100

Finally, a European asylum seeker the *Daily Mail* can't complain about. Kro, as much an Oxford Road establishment as students or rats, has shown us for years that there's more to Denmark than bacon and, erm, oh... It's a cosy little shop, and is usually bustling with undergraduates and their loan-grabbing chums, so it gets pretty full around belly hour. There's a mix of the usual fodder on offer, but you'll find some traditional Danish dishes lurking between the chicken salads and beef burgers.

⊙ *Mon–Fri, 8.30am–11pm; Sat, 10.30am–11pm; Sun, 10.30am–10.30pm; Food, Mon–Sat, 'til 9pm; Sun, 'til 8pm*
⊙ *Roasted root veg hash, £4.50*

Le Mont
Levels 5 and 6 Urbis, Cathedral Gardens
(0161) 605 8282

Ignore the Hitchcockian gatherings of young emo children standing outside the entrance and head up the Urbis elevator to Le Mont. A restaurant overlooking the grand city of Manchester, it's a world away from the dross of Market Street. Creative (but pricey) food guarantees a dinner experience you shouldn't forget. The only improvement they could make would be to pour water onto the local youth below. At least then the whiny brats would have something to moan about.

⊙ *Mon–Fri, 12pm–2.30pm & 7pm–10.30pm; Sat, 7pm–10.30pm*
⊙ *Loin of lamb, £21*
⊙ *£19.95*

Lotus Bar and Dim Sum
35a King Street
(0161) 832 9724

Newbie restaurants usually don't get it right first time. Like Bambi, they take time to get used to their legs and it's a while before they start frolicking around in the woods with the other restaurants. The guys behind Lotus apparently never watched *Bambi*. A classy establishment with a sophisticated décor, Lotus puts many of Manchester's older Chinese establishments to shame. The food is delicious and the cocktails are an interesting batch. Apparently, Lotus is where East meets West. We'd suggest your hand meets your coat and you get here pronto.

⊙ *Mon–Sat, 11am–11.30pm; Sun, 11.30am–9pm*
⊙ *Aromatic crispy duck, £8.80*

Eat

Malmaison Brasserie
1 Gore Street, Piccadilly
(0161) 278 1001

Robert Langdon sat down at a table at Malmaison Brasserie. 'I'm in a restaurant', he thought. After his astonishing adventures in Rome and Paris, the professor needed something to eat. 'Professor means that I teach things', Langdon decided. He imagined himself back in Harvard, standing in front of his class. 'Food goes in your mouth', he would tell the class. Back in Malmaison, there was no priceless artwork for Langdon to examine, but he enjoyed the Renaissance style of the restaurant anyway. 'I have to put the food in my mouth', he reminded himself.

Mon–Fri, 7am–10am & 6pm–11pm; Sat–Sun, 7am–11am & 6pm–11pm

Grilled swordfish, £12.50

The Olive Press
4 Lloyds Street
(0161) 832 9090

As any overpaid food critic will tell you, atmosphere is everything in a restaurant. Atmosphere and good food. Atmosphere, good food and a nice wine list. Atmosphere, good food, a nice wine list and classy service. Sadly, we're neither overpaid, nor your typical food critic per se, so don't take our opinion as gospel, but thankfully, you don't have to be either to enjoy the Olive Press. Good Italian nosh, a laid-back mood and a grand wine selection make this a worthy addition to the Itchy restaurant canon. Plus there's a nice bar. Which explains why we're poor.

Mon–Thu, 11.45am–10pm; Fri–Sat, 11.45am–11pm; Sun, 12pm–9pm

Margherita pizza, £6.50

DELICATESSEN

MANCHESTER'S FAVOURITE DELI

- Olive has everything you could possibly want and much more...from the basics to the unusual and the totally fabulous.
- Fantastic Illy coffees, organic, vegetarian and fairtrade foods from around the world.
- Extensive range of delicious deli sandwiches, salads and hot and cold snacks with a difference.
- Amazing range of beers, wines, champagnes and spirits.
- 40 different types of vodkas - our selection has to be seen to be believed.

We look forward to seeing you soon!

Opening Times: Mon–Fri, 8.00am–10.00pm & Weekends, 9.00am–10.00pm

2 MINUTES FROM UMIST UNI • WHERE SACKVILLE ST AND WHITWORTH ST CROSS
REGENCY HOUSE • 36-38 WHITWORTH STREET • (0161) 236 2360

www.itchymanchester.co.uk

Eat

Rhubarb
167 Burton Road, West Didsbury
(0161) 448 8887

Sometimes wanky restaurants get loads of undeserved praise, with reviewers focusing on arty interiors, wooden floors, and cooing over dishes you can't pronounce. Rhubarb has all of the above, but with the added advantage of deserving all the praise it gets; it really is bloody marvellous. It's cosy and private, and the staff are nice, the food is dribble-worthy and they keep pretension to a minimum. Go for a date, take your parents, or even go alone, and save room for pudding. What a pudding...

Mon–Sat, 5pm–10pm; Sun, 1pm–8.30pm
Hot sticky date pudding with toffee sauce and vanilla ice cream, £5.95
£11.95

Royal Orchid
36 Charlotte Street
(0161) 236 5183

Chinatown can be a dazzling affair for the first-timer. Thousands of different Chinese restaurants vying for your attention can be a tad overwhelming. Many people get scared and run to Tesco to pick up a ready-meal. We don't like to see this happen, if only for the fact that we live off that microwaveable gold and if you steal it all, we have to eat cold noodles. And bark. To stop this cruelty to Itchy writers, pledge to visit the Royal Orchid. It's a SuperTed of a restaurant and will quite leave you full, content, and laughing at the days when you used to steal our food.

Mon–Thu, 12pm–2.30pm & 5.30pm–11pm; Fri, 12pm–11pm; Sun, 1pm–10.30pm
Spicy Thai fish cakes, £5.50

Food for nought

We like getting things free. As we've recently gotten on first name basis with our repossession man, getting things for free is a necessity. Thankfully, Manchester has a variety of places for us to pick up a free bit of grub. No more pot noodles for us. If you feel lucky, **Revolution** (90-94 Oxford Road) are the brave owners of a 15 minute wait or your meal is free policy. Hit it in peak hours if you want to improve your chances of smugly leaving the restaurant with a full wallet. You might be able to blag your way into one of the many taster evenings that occur around Manchester. New restaurants need willing volunteers to try out their shiny new menus, so keep an eye out for these free evenings. www.itchycity.co.uk will keep you in the loop.

Eat

Siam Orchid
52–54 Portland Street
(0161) 236 1388

No matter how stony-faced they may appear in public, give someone a stage, a microphone and the words to Robbie Williams's *Angels* and you'll see a whole new side to them. Probably a worse one. The Siam Orchid, aside from offering a karaoke night to budding *X Factor* fodder, is a darn nice restaurant. The food is apologetically inexpensive and tastes about as good as you'd like it to. It's the karaoke that cements its place in the Itchy guide though. Everyone likes to pretend they're Ol' Blue Eyes, don't they?

Mon–Fri, 12pm–2.30pm & 5pm–11.30pm; Sat–Sun, 5pm–11.30pm
Green curry, £6.95

Tampopo
16 Albert Square
(0161) 819 1966

Generally, new things scare people. Old biddies think the internet steals their souls. George Bush thinks reusable energy is the work of the devil. Jonathan Ross is scared of funny jokes. Thankfully, the folk behind Tampopo are a fearless bunch. Introducing Manchester to the delights of Vietnamese cuisine, this is a refreshing eating experience. Try a variety of food you've never heard of. Laugh as you sit next to a complete stranger at the long tables. Mock George Bush and old people. Eating out has never been so much fun.

Mon–Sat, 12pm–11pm; Sun, 12pm–10pm
Chicken ramen soup, £7.95
£11.95

Teppanyaki
58–60 George Street
(0161) 228 2219

Some haiku to Teppanyaki:
The brave chef stands tall
Makes meals for the customers
In front of their eyes.
Teppanyaki serves
Great food but tad expensive;
A meal with strangers.
Not that weird to do.
Honestly we swear on it.
You might make new friends.
Go to this venue.
Be brave oh Itchy readers.
Sure beats KFC.

Mon–Fri, 12pm–2pm & 6pm–11pm; Sat, 6pm–11pm
Beef sashimi, £9.90

www.itchymanchester.co.uk

Eat

Try Thai
50 Faulkner Street
(0161) 228 2218

We're absolute pushovers. Whenever we get asked to do something, whenever Carol Vorderman gives us her 'get a loan' eyes, whenever someone asks us to get drunk, we can't help but say yes. Therefore, upon spying its neon sign, you can imagine how we rushed through the doors at Try Thai. Usually, we regret such decisions. However, this time, the gods of impulsiveness were with us. We're glad we tried Thai. If someone opened a Try Beer establishment, we don't think we'd be able to resist.

🕒 *Mon–Thu, 12pm–11pm; Fri–Sat, 12pm–12am; Sun, 12pm–10pm*
🍴 *Sweet and sour chicken, £7.50*

Umami
149 Oxford Road
(0161) 273 2300

Despite living with the daily threat of being flooded by a leak in the Aquatics Centre, the underground Umami is a thoroughly laid-back place to eat. Modern décor, plus attentive and caring staff mean that if you should ever find yourself trapped in this no man's land between the two university campuses, you should have a nice little foxhole to run into if the rivalry descends into full-blown warfare. The food is a mix of traditional Japanese cuisine with a selection of accessible dishes lobbed in for the more committed bacon buttie eaters. Going underground has never been so much fun.

🕒 *Mon–Sat, 12pm–11pm; Sun, 12pm–10pm*
🍴 *Lunch express menu, £4.95*

Eat

Wagamama
1a The Printworks
(0161) 839 5916

What once was the lowly grub of the student classes has been restored to its former glory as an Eastern delicacy. Behold how the noodle is revered in Wagamama. Reclaimed from the insides of microwaves and Pot Noodle cartons, and topped with a medley of delicious Japanese foods, it is no longer a snack for between lunch and dinner but, lo, a meal in its own right. Praise the mighty noodle. Praise Wagamama – servers of the mighty noodle. Praise their communal seating arrangement, eating next to complete strangers on benches.

- *Mon–Sat, 12pm–11pm; Sun, 12pm–10pm*
- *Mandarin and chicken salad, £7.95*
- *£11.25*

Yang Sing
34 Princess Street
(0161) 236 2200

It's hard to believe this restaurant is 30 years of age. In restaurant years, you'd expect it to be thinking of retiring and settling down to life as a pensioner. Thankfully though, Yang Sing is far away from its dotage. This Cantonese restaurant is one of Manchester's premium venues for everything dim sum related and keeps itself as fresh as air. A grandiose menu to satisfy even the pickiest terracotta army, Yang Sing has space for 250 hungry punters, so expect it to be lively – a quiet Friday night meal this is not.

- *Sun–Thu, 12pm–11.45pm; Fri–Sat, 12pm–12.15am*
- *Banquet, £25 per person*

Zen Zero
202 Burton Road
(0161) 434 2777

Unless there's a sudden zombie outbreak in the centre of Manchester, there isn't really much of a reason to make for West Didsbury. However, if you do find yourself plagued by the undead and Zen Zero is en-route to your shopping-mall/safe-haven of choice then you could do a lot worse than to hole up here. Presuming it's still open. Winner of many a coveted award, the food is grade-A fare and the restaurant is nicely decorated. Plus you can see all the exits and entrances – useful when dining under the shadow of a zombie apocalypse.

- *Mon–Thu, 12pm–10.30pm; Fri–Sat, 12pm–11pm*
- *Duck breast, £14.50*

www.itchymanchester.co.uk

Test of moral fibre

ALRIGHT, SO WE'RE ALL SUPPOSED TO BE EATING ETHICALLY NOWADAYS. BUT WHAT WE WANT TO KNOW IS WHETHER ANY OF THE MONKEYS THAT BANG ON ABOUT THIS STUFF HAVE EVER TRIED IT OUT WHEN PICKING UP SOME POST-PUB STOMACH FILLERS. IT'S A BLOODY NIGHTMARE. OBSERVE:

Illustration by Si Clark, www.si-clark.co.uk

1 Food miles – According to some environmental fascist or other, it's not ecologically friendly to eat stuff that's been flown across the world when you could chomp on courgettes grown much closer to home. Not according to our friendly burger van, however.

Itchy: 'Excuse me, but how many food miles has that quarter pounder done?'

Burger man: 'What?'

Itchy: 'How many miles has it travelled to end up here?'

Burger man: 'Ten miles, mate. Straight from Lidl to this spot.'

Itchy: 'But what about where it came from originally? What about the sourcing?'

Burger man: 'Saucing? I've got ketchup and mustard, you cheeky sod. And it's free, not like him down the road and his "10p-a-sachet" bollocks, now you gonna buy this burger or what?'

'Reckon you could catch enough fish for all the UK's chippies using a fishing rod?'

2 Sustainability – It's not meant to be the done thing to eat fish caught in a way that stops our scaly friends reproducing fast enough to prevent their numbers dropping. Sadly, no-one's told our local chippy.

Itchy: 'Is your cod line-caught?'

Chippy owner: 'Yeah, it's caught mate. How else do you reckon it comes from the sea?'

Itchy: 'No, I'm asking if it was caught using a fishing rod.'

Chippy owner: 'You reckon you could catch enough fish for all the UK's chippies using a fishing rod?'

Itchy: 'Erm, no...'

Chippy owner: 'Right, well there's your answer then.'

Itchy: '...but, you know that you should only really eat fish from sustainable sources don't you?'

Chippy owner: 'Oh yeah? According to who? The media? Reckon all that coke they're on's organic? Produced locally, is it?'

Itchy: 'Well, it's not always possible to consume entirely ethically...'

Chippy owner: 'My point exactly. One cod and chips then is it?'

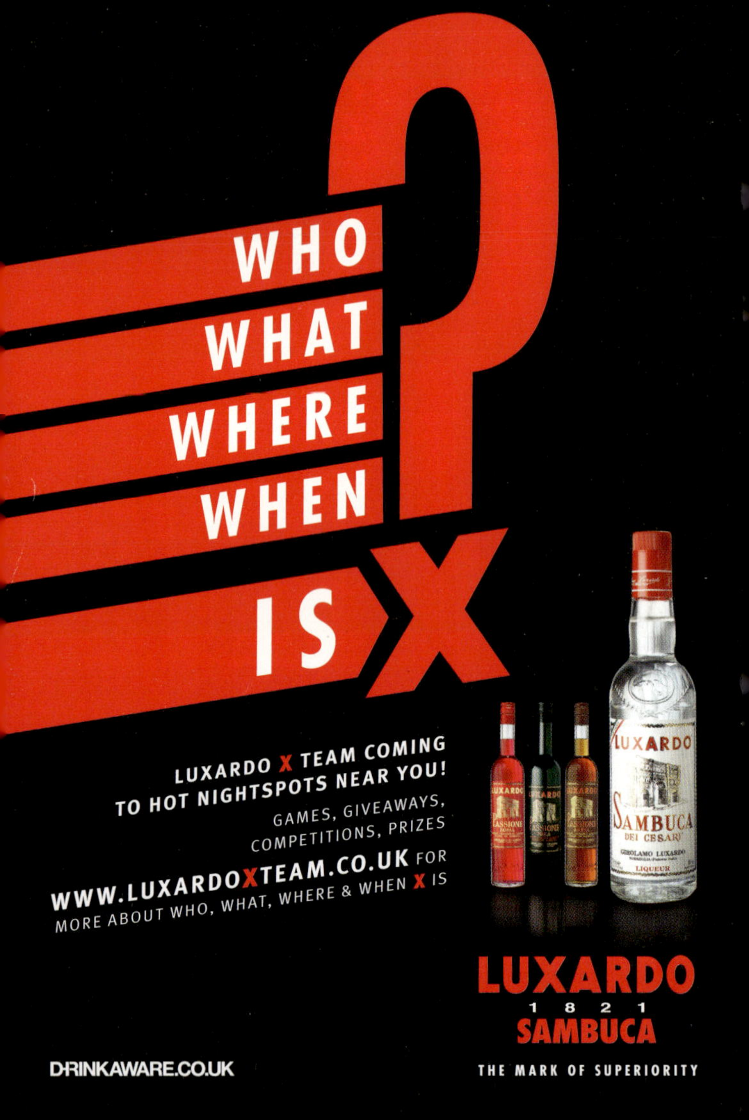
WHO
WHAT
WHERE
WHEN
IS X
LUXARDO X TEAM COMING
TO HOT NIGHTSPOTS NEAR YOU!
GAMES, GIVEAWAYS,
COMPETITIONS, PRIZES
WWW.LUXARDOXTEAM.CO.UK FOR
MORE ABOUT WHO, WHAT, WHERE & WHEN X IS
LUXARDO
SAMBUCA
DEI CESARI
GIROLAMO LUXARDO
LIQUEUR
LUXARDO
1 8 2 1
SAMBUCA
THE MARK OF SUPERIORITY
DRINKAWARE.CO.UK

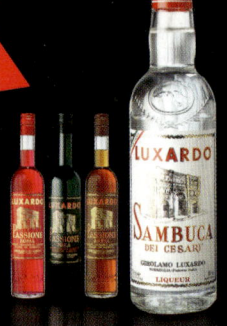

Drink

Drink

CASTLEFIELD BARS

Atlas
376 Deansgate
(0161) 834 2124

Thankfully, Atlas has yet to catch the viral infection of irritating people from the bars of the Locks. A smart-casual bar, this is a mile away from loud-mouthed children 'living for the weekend'. It's a comfortable environment where you can chat away the evening – don't expect loud music and DJs that talk over their tunes. This is a place to unwind slowly without the need to shell out for a £5.99 whale song CD. Bring some friends, catch up and think about how great it would be if all bars were like this.

Mon–Thu, 12pm–11pm; Fri–Sat, 12pm–2am; Sun, 12pm–10.30pm

Knott Bar
374 Deansgate
(0161) 839 9299

The Knott spot-it game: If you spot a scally, a couple under an umbrella, a stray dog, drunk men singing football chants, then award yourself five points. If you spot a horse and cart, a lost student, a collection of lost students, a couple having a drunken fight, award yourself ten points. If you spot someone sitting in Knott and realising that this review tells them nothing about the actual bar except that it has large windows, award yourself fifteen points. If you spot aforementioned person throwing Itchy guide across the room in disgust, award yourself a free Itchy guide.

Sun–Wed, 12pm–11pm; Thu, 12pm–12am; Fri–Sat, 12pm–1am

Barca
Arches 8 & 9 Catalan Square
(0161) 839 7099

When the first noise that greets your ears as you enter a bar is the sound of the bar staff sighing, you know there's something amiss. As they lethargically pull your pint and gaze longingly at the clock, you get the impression that the Barca staff would rather be at the other side of the bar – at least there they'd have something to do. This place fills out nicely at weekends, but catch it on any working evening and it's a doornail. As you pick up your coat and the barman turns off the light behind you, you've got to wonder if it was really worth the wonky trek through the cobbled streets…

Mon–Thu, 12pm–11pm; Fri–Sat, 12pm–2am; Sun, 12pm–10.30pm

Drink

CASTLEFIELD PUBS

Dukes 92
Castle Street
(0161) 839 8646
Like its namesake, the very lock that prevents us all from drowning in shopping trolleys and used connies, Dukes 92 filters out the dross. As you sit and savour your well-earned pint (unless you actually live there Castlefield is a right trek to get to), you can imagine horses pulling boats along the canals and gentrified types crowded around the fine seating, discussing commerce. Your conversation about McLaren's back four could prove to be just as weighty, 'cos now you have class.
Mon–Sat, 11am–11pm;
Sun, 12pm–10.30pm

The White Lion
43 Liverpool Road, Castlefield
(0161) 832 7373
Time Team may as well be standing outside with a bucket and spade, since this pub is buried in so much history. Although rest assured, if they ever try to excavate under our favourite boozer, we'd be first to set up a picket line. Standing in the same spot for over two centuries hasn't made the White Lion a place for old punters though, and you'll regularly find young urbanites here, clambering for a taste of their country upbringing. The outdoor area is a bit special, although if you spot a couple of roman coins protruding from the soil, don't tell that Robinson fella.
Mon–Sat, 12pm–11pm;
Sun, 12pm–10.30pm

The Ox Hotel
71 Liverpool Road
(0161) 839 7740
Sadly not named after a large and masculine plough-pulling beast, but rather a common day spud, the Ox Hotel is no small potato. The comfortable atmosphere would make King Edward feel at home, while the selection of proper drinks has more or less anything you could Desiree and is fit for a Jersey Royal. Take it steady though, since you wouldn't want to get mashed and end up dancing out of town behind a pied Maris Piper. Just don't mention the, ahem, famine, and certainly don't ask the obvious question – why didn't they just eat something else?
Mon–Sat, 12pm–11pm;
Sun, 12pm–10.30pm

www.itchymanchester.co.uk

Drink

CHORLTON BARS

The Bar
533 Wilbraham Road
(0161) 881 7576

Not a bad bar but it just doesn't stand out. It has a range of draught beers, meaning you're not paying a tenner for a pint (bloody beer in bottles) and the menu's varied, but something's missing. Maybe it's the mock rustico feel, or the restaurant/café layout, but it left us uninspired. Take friends, and once you're drunk you can make your own atmosphere. It's amazing what you can do with bog roll and some sticky-back plastic.

- *Mon–Sat, 11am–11pm; Sun, 12pm–3pm & 7pm–10.30pm; Food, 12pm–8pm*
- *Bangers and mash, £7.95*
- *£6.95*

Urulu
398 Barlow Moor Road
(0161) 881 6789

Don't mistake this place for a naff theme bar, no, no, no, this is a place where real Aussies go for real Aussie food and real Aussie beers (either that or they import them to add that truly authentic feel to the place). It's a good menu, and the beer lineup is good, plus its not a bad place to sit with a kangaroo burger and ponder how much better life would be if you were soaking up the Aussie sun, not sat in a bar in Manchester while it dribbles down outside.

- *Mon–Sat, 9.30am–11pm; Sat–Sun, 10am–11.30pm; Food, Mon–Sat, 9.30am–9pm; Sun, 10am–9pm*
- *Aussie breakfast, £5.95*
- *£8.95*

The Lead Station
99 Beech Road
(0161) 881 5559

Ever since we got our stomachs pumped for chewing on *Star Wars* figurines, we've always been suspicious of things with lead in the title, and The Lead Station does little to allay this very rational fear. It's a bar with an identity crisis. It's a great place to sit and watch the bohemian beauties of Chorlton pass you by, but not really the kind of place to 'go large' on a Saturday night. We make a plea to The Lead Station – decide what you want to be and stick to it, please.

- *Mon–Fri, 11am–11pm; Sat, 10am–11pm; Sun, 10am–10pm; Food, Mon–Sat, 11am–10pm; Sun, 10am–9.30pm*
- *Poached salmon sandwich, £3.95*
- *£9.95*

Drink

CHORLTON PUBS

The Beech Inn
72 Beech Road, Chorlton
(0161) 881 1180

If Itchy had a pint for every traditional pub we've been into, Itchy would be, well, drunkety drunk drunk, to be honest. Nevertheless, we ventured into The Beech with a smile and a couple of buddies to prop us up. Sadly, The Beech is a bit like going back to school. It's tiny, old men brush past you a little too often and it's very cold. This place is not for the meek, nor the drunk, but it's worth a drop in, especially if you like older guys. Maybe we can start a dating service – those with their own teeth need not apply.

Mon–Thu, 11am–10.30pm; Fri–Sat, 11am–12.30am; Sun, 11am–10.30pm

The Horse and Jockey
9 Chorlton Green, Chorlton
(0161) 881 6494

Come with us on a journey… enter the mock-Tudor vortex. Notice how all of the moisture leaves your eyeballs in a vain attempt to protect your brain from damage. Take a seat on a rickety and possibly pissed-on stool while we order you a pint of dirty ale. Drink in the fetid atmosphere and imagine yourself sat on the green outside in the summer, soaking up the fumes from cars that roar around you, possibly mowing down a few small children in their path. Imagine yourself in this tranquil oasis and remember, it's not snobby to wonder why your stool is damp.

Mon–Thu, 12pm–11pm; Fri–Sat, 12pm–12am; Sun, 12pm–11pm

The Famous Trevor Arms
135 Beech Road, Chorlton
(0161) 881 8209

This place manages to be both completely comforting and completely depressing all at the same time, an accomplishment we think deserves some kudos. Trev has a large selection of beer and ales (which are fairly cheap considering it's on the swanky Beech Road), and a wicked selection of bar games to while away the hours, which should mean a Sunday afternoon in this place would be the perfect antidote to weekend liver poisoning… but only if you're a local. All the trendy Chorltonites are better off elsewhere – find a wine bar and stay there.

Mon–Thu, 11am–11pm; Fri–Sat, 11am–12am; Sun, 12pm–11am

Marble Beer House
57 Manchester Road, Chorlton
(0161) 881 9206

Well, Marble Beer House, here we are, together again at last after all this time. So what do you have to say for yourself then eh? Now don't try to hide it. We've all noticed the standards of the beer slipping, don't think you can pull the wool over our eyes. Have you no dignity, Marble Beer House? Your only saving grace was your beer and now, now you've gone and ruined that too. Why, oh why? We could have been something, you know. We could have made beautiful music in the wee small hours but you blew it, and we can never forgive you.

Mon–Sat, 12pm–11pm; Sun, 12pm–10.30pm

www.itchymanchester.co.uk

Drink

CITY CENTRE BARS

Che

4–5 Portland Street
(0161) 236 4511

'Motorcycle diaries. Monday 23rd, 1951. The wheel keeps on falling off my sodding scooter. Sancho blames the weather. I blame the damn capitalists. I dream of a world where all men, even ugly ones, can live equally. When I'm done making a perfect society, I'm going to set up a bar. In Manchester. Because once I'm poster boy to the entire student demographic, I'm going to be able to do shit like that.'

Mon-Tue, 12pm–12am; Wed-Sat, 12pm–2am; Food, Mon-Sat, 12pm–9pm
Chicken tapas, £4.45
£13.95

Fab Café

111 Portland Street
(0161) 236 2019

Fab Café is a kitsch and colourful shrine to all things cult. From the endless movie memorabilia to the life-sized Dalek (thankfully restrained behind a small fence – phew) and the retro arcade games, Fab Café sits happily at the cool end of the geek spectrum. Which is strange as none of the ladies seem impressed by our complete collection of *Pokémon* cards. What? We were told to catch 'em all. They're blatantly just jealous. As are you. Stay away from our *Pokémon* cards if you know what's good for you…

Mon-Thu, 4.45pm–2am; Fri-Sat, 3.30pm–2am; Sun, 6pm–12.30am
Fri-Sat, £2 after 10pm

Tribeca brings New York Attic Chic to Manchester

Tribeca Bar & BED… a chic and vibrant city centre bar in the heart of Manchester, with a distinct and sophisticated New York air. The bar offers a relaxed atmosphere by day, and a buzzy, vibrant scene by night. A mix of raw tunes and fresh cocktails. Welcome to our ultra lounge.

House Wine only £5 a bottle!! *Daily from 4-8pm Rosé £6 a bottle*

Tribeca Bar & BED, 50 Sackville Street, Manchester M1 3WF
tel **0161 236 8300** web **www.tribeca-bar.co.uk**

Drink

Kro Piccadilly
1 Piccadilly Gardens
(0161) 224 5765

As the Thunderbird 2 of the Kro family, Kro Piccadilly is the biggest, the brightest and the most versatile of the lot. Sure, it won't be at the disaster site first, and it won't get you up to the space station. But who wants to go to that stupid space station anyway? What did Quasimodo Tracey get up to in there all day? Anyway, Kro Piccadilly has a good atmosphere, delightful food and if you need a pint at half eleven of a morning, it's pretty much cornered the market.

Mon–Thu, 8am–12am; Fri–Sat, 8am–2am; Sun, 8am–11pm; Food, Mon–Sun, 8.30am–9.30pm
Chicken schnitzel, £9.80
£9.50

Tribeca
50 Sackville Street
(0161) 236 8300

'Tribeca' stands for the location 'Triangle Beneath Canal', not the pac-a-mac and minimiser bra-sporting 'Tribe of C&A', or the massively well-endowed cross-dresser 'Tripod Rebecca', though staff here are so outstandingly friendly that they'd welcome you if you were either. Along with the club and restaurant below, this New York loft-style bar is a real old mate of Itchy's, with great drinks deals, even greater attitude and consistently fresh nights. Forget triangles – this is a top all-rounder. Be there or be square.

Mon, Wed–Thu, 12pm–1am; Tue, 12pm–2am; Fri–Sat, 12pm–2.30am; Sun, 12pm–12.30am

Mojo
19 Back Bridge Street
(0161) 839 5330

If Mojo were a person, it would be Hendrix. If it were a piece of furniture, it would be a revolving leopardskin bed. Item of clothing? Easy. Bruce Springsteen's Levis. But as it stands, Mojo is a bar. And what a bar it is. Perfectly blending rock 'n' roll with soul and funk, Mojo is a grown-up, laid-back indie club with a terrific cocktail list and an atmosphere that would scream 'effortlessly cool' in neon letters if it could be bothered. It's not the most roomy of establishments, however, so leave the attitude and any attachment to your personal space at the door.

Mon–Thu & Sun, 5pm–2am; Fri–Sat, 5pm–3am

www.itchymanchester.co.uk

Drink

CITY CENTRE PUBS

The Athenaeum
1 York Street
(0161) 819 1055

So it took us six tries to spell the name of this pub correctly, but we're not going to hold that against them, because it's actually quite a nice place. And we like a good pint better than anger. A grandiose venue with a crackling atmosphere, there's a large selection of drinkables and the staff are polite and friendly. They even trade us beer for monetary valuables. Now if we could only spell the name. We're not stupid, we just got kidnapped before our GCSEs and forced into slave labour by Itchy's editor.
Mon–Sat, 11am–11pm;
Sun, 12pm–10.30pm

The Bridge
58 Bridge Street
(0161) 834 0242

Until recently, it was the finest gastropub in town, but it's recently been taken over by the company behind The Brunswick on Piccadilly, so who knows what the future holds for The Bridge? Unpretentious and honest, if a little pricey in truth, this pub is located and named after a catastrophic bridge collapse in 1831. Which is a cheery thought isn't it? If they take the locally-sourced black pudding off the menu, there'll be riots in the streets of Manchester. Or there should be. Not that we are encouraging rioting, maybe just severe tutting.
Mon–Sat, 12pm–11pm;
Sun, 12pm–10.30pm

The Bank
55 Mosley Street
(0161) 228 7560

If you're looking for a loan, then you've come to the wrong place. If you're looking to walk away with a bag full of insurance bonds, then leave now. Basically, we're telling you that The Bank isn't really a bank. Barclays is up the road. If you walked in with a desire for a nice city pub, then you've hit the proverbial jackpot. It's a pleasant place, as demonstrated by the fact that the hard working 9–5ers choose this place to catch a sneaky pint during lunch. A word of warning though: be prepared to see a couple of scallies with tights over their heads anyway.
Mon–Sat, 12pm–11pm;
Sun, 12pm–10.30pm

Drink

Britons Protection
50 Great Bridgewater Street
(0161) 236 5895

Quite what this pub protects us Brits from is somewhat of a mystery; we don't think it's an embassy, and we somewhat doubt its jurisdictional credentials. Nevertheless, if we were being chased by a bunch of angry Argentinians then this would be our first port of call. Not for sanctuary you understand, but rather because we'd buy them a drink to calm them down. They'd remark how they enjoyed the classy interior. They'd comment on the 200-plus range of whiskies. They'd pat us on the back and forgive us for stealing their chickens, for a while anyway.

Mon–Sat, 12pm–11pm;
Sun, 12pm–10.30pm

Sir Ralph Abercrombie
35 Bootle Street
(0161) 834 1807

Oh, those were the days, when knighthoods weren't awarded on the merits of how much one earned on television. The Sir Ralph Abercrombie stands in memory of a famed Napoleonic general, and with a beer garden Lord Nelson would be proud of, this is an old-fashioned boozer, complete with a splendid range of tasty real ale. Supposedly, this 200-year-old pub is haunted by a chap bumped off during the 1891 Peterloo Massacre. History buffs can see this battle recreated every other weekend outside the Manchester City ground.

Mon–Sat, 12pm–11pm;
Sun, 12pm–10.30pm

The Old Wellington Inn
New Cathedral Gate
(0161) 830 1440

The Welly is a fine drinking experience, although you may have to battle your way through the shoppers during the weekend or slalom through the outdoor beer garden with your plastic pint pot. Oh, how we abhor those. Although it was reconstructed piece by piece after the bomb of 1996, this little boozer dates back to the 1500's. This probably explains the extra low ceilings; giants or people with impressive mohawks should avoid.

Mon–Sat, 11am–11pm; Sun,
12pm–10.30pm; Food, Mon–Sat,
11.30am–9pm; Sun, 12pm–5pm
Fillet of beef, £14.95
£10

Waxy O'Connor's
The Printworks, Corporation Street
(0161) 835 1210

You'd think people didn't want us to go to Ireland. Basing our assumptions of the land of leprechauns on Waxy O' Connors, Ireland must be crowded, not very well decorated and full of suspiciously young-looking boozers from Manchester. The Irish tourist board must have a struggle basing a marketing campaign on that. Waxy's is your typical Printworks fare. If you understand what we're on about, you're ok. If you're a newbie and haven't a clue what this means, you'll soon get the idea. Keep your wallet close and your beer closer.

Mon–Wed, 12pm–11pm; Thu,
12pm–12am; Fri–Sat, 12pm–1am;
Sun 12pm–10.30pm

www.itchymanchester.co.uk

Drink

DEANSGATE BARS

Life Café
23 Peter Street
(0161) 833 3000

If you are a fan of *Upstairs, Downstairs*, you'll appreciate Life Café. In the heaving bar above, clueless landed gentry make scoffing noises and peruse the cricket scores. Downstairs, in the dank Late Room, their proletarian cousins jig and get drunk, happy in the knowledge that although they may not have the fancy clothes of those above, they are not wankers. Itchy is a big fan of Club Biscuit on a Friday. We just wish they had some custard creams behind the bar.

Mon–Thu, 12pm–10.30pm;
Fri, 12pm–2am; Sat, 5pm–2am

Loaf
Arches 3a–5 Deansgate Locks
(0161) 819 5858

Fashion victims, weekend millionaires and potential *Big Brother* contestants jostle for position, controlled by door staff that let women in on bra size and men on how easily they reckon they could extract you internal organs with their bare hands if they get bored later on. Yet for all of this it's still incredibly busy. People for some reason actually want to go. When we rule the world, we're going to make all the people that went here write us a letter of apology. In a world where mullets are acceptable, Loaf is king. Now where's Macbeth when you need him?

Mon–Tue, 12pm–12.30am; Wed–Sat, 12pm–2am; Sun, 12pm–10.30pm

The Living Room
80 Deansgate
(0161) 832 0083

If your living room was full of the people who drink here, you'd probably move or consider finding yourself a new social circle. Alas, the Living Room is still one of the most popular bars in Manchester and, we're reluctant to add, a city centre institution. If the daytime crowd is ladies who lunch, the evening crowd is ladies who want to. Itchy once saw ex-Man Utd plodder Nicky Butt in here. He had a leather shirt on.

Mon–Wed, 10am–12am; Thu, 5pm–1am;
Fri–Sat, 5pm–2am; Sun, 5pm–10.30pm;
Food, Mon–Sat, 12pm–9.30pm;
Sun, 6pm–9.30pm

🍴 Roast lamb cutlets, £14.50

💷 £13.75

Panacea Bar & Restaurant
14 John Dalton Street
(0161) 833 0000

Certainly not an answer to all your city centre night out problems, but not bad if you are feeling swanky. Come one, come all, said the management when this ultra smart bar opened. We're no snobs, they reckoned. They were lying. Unless you mind being judged on looks, class and wealth with every move, you may feel as if you've forgotten to wear any trousers. One for a glass of champers before moving to the excellent Restaurant Bar and Grill upstairs, perhaps.

Mon–Sat, 12pm–2am; Sun, 4pm–12am;
Food, Mon–Sat, 12pm–10.30pm

🍴 Fish and chips, £13

💷 £8 per glass

Drink

DEANSGATE PUBS

Mr Thomas's Chop House
52 Cross Street
(0161) 832 2245

Not just chops, but an array of good, uncomplicated British food is on offer in this famous city centre pub. A popular Saturday retreat for hen-pecked husbands, it relieves stress, knots in feet and the memory of Primark. Down points include occasional spectacularly bad service, and the side door leading to a pretty alley that doubles as a toilet on a Friday and Saturday night.

Mon–Fri, 11.30am–3pm & 5.30pm–9.30pm; Sat, 11.30am–4pm & 5.30pm–9.30pm; Sun, 12pm–4pm & 5.30pm–9.30pm
Corn beef hash, £12.95
£12

The Old Nags Head
19 Jacksons Row
(0161) 832 4315

An old school pub with rubbish fruit machines, sticky carpets and karaoke on a Friday or Saturday night. If you have a few too many and decide that you do know the way to Amarillo, the assembled company probably won't mind that much. It's like the local pub you never knew existed. We occasionally yearn for the traditional pubs of the countryside, and the Old Nag's Head is a gem in an area more renowned for its rather large lumps of coal.

Mon–Sat, 12pm–11pm; Sun, 12pm–10.30pm

The Old Grapes
Little Quay Street
(0161) 839 4359

Famously owned by *Corrie*'s Vera Duckworth, the Grapes is a city centre institution and popular post work meeting place, although it's definitely more Battersby than Baldwin. You may even see the odd cast member in there, swapping the dubious-looking gravy browning of the Rovers Return for a selection of proper ales. Though if you do spy one, please try to control yourselves and not lick their faces. You don't know who's been there before you. And, um, you know, it's rude. Yes, Itchy readers, we're like the prudish father you never had.

Mon–Sat, 12pm–11pm; Sun, 12pm–10.30pm

Sawyer's Arms
138 Deansgate
(0161) 834 2133

An honest drinking man's boozer amid the bars and restaurants on and around Deansgate, although it's probably worth knowing it's a match day stronghold for Man U fans. If it's non-spectacular bangers and mash and a pint you're after, the Sawyers will see you right. You can look at the floor and reminisce about a time when all pub carpets were this viscous. Approach with low expectations to avoid disappointment – we figure it's a lot like a date with us.

Mon–Sat, 12pm–11pm; Sun, 12pm–10.30pm

Get there with system one travelcards.co.uk

www.itchymanchester.co.uk

Drink

DIDSBURY BARS

O'Neill's
655–657 Wilmslow Road
(0161) 448 7941

Ah, teh be sure, thars nuttin qwuite loike a paoint. When we was smaal da' useta feed us the stout from his pot inteh our bottle to aid our slumber. Noaw we're a growed up we take ourself to an autentick Oirish boozer such as O'Neills teh soak in de Oirish atmosphere… ok, this place is as Irish as Warwick Davis in the *Leprechaun* movies, but they do a cracking burger.

- *Mon–Thu, 12pm–11pm; Fri–Sat, 12pm–12am; Sun, 11.30am–11.30pm; Food, Mon–Sat, 12pm–9pm; Sun, 11.30am–8pm*
- *Cheese and bacon burger, £4.95*
- *£7.95*

The Slug and Lettuce
651 Wilmslow Road
(0161) 434 1011

The Didsbury outlet of the well-known 'Slag and Lettuce' chain provides a posh bar and restaurant for older students and professionals alike. It's over 21s only so you can take a night off from dodging Bacardi Breezer-fuelled freshers in the plush interior, and if you're feeling ambitious you can break the bank by spending an entire evening drinking expensive gin and tonic. The food is a regular treat, but like the booze may require you to offload some of your share portfolio.

- *Mon–Sat, 12pm–11pm; Sun, 12pm–10.30pm; Food, Mon–Sun, 12pm–9pm*
- *Cajun chicken fillet burger, £7.95*
- *£14*

Pitcher and Piano
1d School Lane, Didsbury
(0161) 448 9326

Every now and then a venue arrives and we have to admit defeat. Swanky interior on the cheap? Check. Footy screens to draw the richer hooligans? Check. Leather sofas? Check. Short skirts? Check. This place looks good but somewhere along the way it fell foul of its own creation. It's got a naff atmosphere, unless dancing with jailbait WKD drinkers and paying three quid a pint for the privilege is your cup of tea. Itchy no like.

- *Mon–Tue, 12pm–11pm; Wed–Thu, 12pm–11.30pm; Fri–Sat, 12pm–12am; Sun, 12pm–11.30pm; Food, Mon–Sun, 12pm–9pm*
- *Steak and mushroom pie, £9.25*
- *£12.50*

Drink

DIDSBURY PUBS

The Assembly Bar & Grill
4 Lapwing Lane
(0161) 445 3653
Owned by the people behind the Metropolitan, the Assembly is a similarly up-market and relaxed establishment for the West Didsbury set. There's neat little niches for drinking or dining al fresco, and the bar boasts an impressive selection of wines. It ain't cheap, but having said that it's friendly as well as flash.
Mon–Fri, 11.30am–12am; Sat, 10am–12am; Sun, 10am–11.30pm; Food, Mon–Fri, 12pm–4pm & 5.30pm–10pm; Sat, 10am–4pm & 6pm–10pm; Sun, 10am–5pm & 6pm–9.30pm
Organic salmon, £13.95
£11.95

The Metropolitan
2 Lapwing Lane
(0161) 374 9559
There's a sense of 'little London up North' about the Met. You'll struggle to hear a Mancunian accent and the bar prices are more akin to those of the capital than a friendly local. That said, it's busy every day of the week and serves a great roast. And as it's a popular haunt for off-duty doctors, it's a safe place to be too – they'll be lining up to perform the Heimlich manoeuvre should you choke at the bar prices.
Mon–Wed, 11.30am–11.30pm; Thu–Sat, 11.30am–12am; Sun, 12pm–11.30pm; Food, Mon–Thu, 12pm–9.30pm; Fri–Sat, 12pm–10pm; Sun, 12pm–9pm
Metropolitan burger, £8.50
£13.50

The Dog & Patridge
667 Wilmslow Road, Didsbury
(0161) 434 3078
'When I was young, I never needed any one, and making love was just for fun <sigh>, those days are gone... la la oooohh...' sorry, distracted there. See, we went to the Dog and we had a fab time – it's a proper pub with proper beer and wooden floors so that they can wash the spit and sawdust away, and it's cosy and not too smelly. This is the kind of pub that makes you want to go for a walk just so you can sit inside it with your muddy boots feeling all smug that you earned your pint. Just a damn shame about the music – surely Celine Dion is a step too far into madness.
Mon–Thu, 11am–11pm; Fri–Sat, 11am–12.30am; Sun, 11am–11.30pm

The Station
682 Wilmslow Road
(0161) 445 9761
Among all the wine bar bistros and chain pubs of Didsbury village, the Station is a sweet little sigh of relief. This local pub for local people is free from the shackles of the breweries who have strangled the life out of the ale houses of this country. It's a friendly pub where you can (at last) get a good pint of Guinness and watch the football, without having to endure all the drunken students doing the Didsbury dozen. If you do run into a group of pissed up rugby-playing scholars, just make sure you've got a waterproof handy. They're not just for flume rides.
Mon–Thu, 11am–11pm; Fri, 11am–12am; Sat, 11am–1am; Sun, 12pm–10.30pm

www.itchymanchester.co.uk

41

Drink

FALLOWFIELD BARS

Bar XS
343 Wilmslow Road
(0161) 257 2403

Thanks to the wise decision not to play on the place's past as a train station and concentrate on the entertainment instead, Bar XS is rather unremarkable, consistently providing average drinks at average prices in average surroundings. Comedy fans are well catered for though, with weekly stand-up night XS Malarkey every Tuesday, and karaoke on Thursday, usually offering stuck-in-the-baggy-era locals the opportunity to showcase their 'unique' take on *I Am The Resurrection*.
Sun–Thu, 12pm–2am; Fri–Sat, 12pm–3am
Tue, £4; Thu, £2

Glass
258 Wilmslow Road
(0161) 257 0770

Glass has identity issues. Oddly ashamed to be pigeonholed as a shots bar (various combinations of curdled brightly-coloured alcoholic goop can be yours for a very reasonable pound a go), it tries to disguise itself as something of a funky lounge-bar affair. The sort of place you might go to sip a mojito and talk about the fickle nature of the salesman's existence. 'Quirky' retro-esque seating and a host of surprisingly credible nights ranging from house to live comedy may lend it an air of respectability, but all the while it just can't give up those sticky, sickly shots.
Mon–Sat, 12pm–12am;
Sun, 12pm–10.30pm

GIVE IT A SHOT PROMOTION

When it comes to delicious, laid-back drinks, are your shots on target?

If you want to fix a mix that looks and tastes sexy,
try Luxardo's new and adventurous 'Shotails'.
These layered lovelies need just four chilled magic bullets: Luxardo's top notch black and white sambucas, zesty Limoncello, and fiery cranberry Passione Rossa.

For the catsuit-coloured classic Kill Bill Shotail, created for the film's party, simply slip 25ml of Luxardo Passione Nera black sambuca over the same amount of Luxardo Limoncello.

Make the ultimate Revenge (best served cold) with 25ml of classic Luxardo sambuca, topped with 25ml of Passione Rossa, and check out
www.LuxardoXTeam.co.uk
for more Shotail ideas.

LUXARDO 1821 SAMBUCA
THE MARK OF SUPERIORITY

Drink

Snook
317 Wilmslow Road
(0161) 248 0546

Snook is a bar that's too cool to put its name above the door. We suspect this is because it wanted to be one of those hidden away kind of places – the kind that you just have to know about. Unfortunately it finds itself plonked, not very exclusively at all, right on Wilmslow road, so it's forced to compensate. When the self-congratulatory glow of finding the place wears off, there's also porn thoughtfully projected onto the wall just so that regulars can feel smug for understanding it as an ironic post-modern statement on societal hang-ups about female sexuality. Maybe.

Mon–Thu, 8pm–1am; Fri–Sat, 8pm–2am; Sun, 8pm–10.30pm

Trof
2a Landcross Road
(0161) 224 0467

Like a paper company planting new trees, Trof seems committed to repairing the damage it causes. Guilt-stricken about tempting you every evening with its unrelenting programme of quality music nights, top-notch beers, and relaxed atmosphere, this former terrace house tries desperately to atone the next day by assuming a café alter ego. 'I'm sorry,' it says, 'I only wanted you to have some fun. Come back for some hearty, hangover-curing grub. How about a fry-up? Vegetarian if you like? And maybe a hair of the dog?'

Mon–Sun, 9am–12am
Chargrilled tuna steak, £8.95
£6

Décor blimey

Pub décor – boring, eh? Not always. **The Cornerhouse** (0161 228 7621) probably keeps Dulux in business. Regularly splashing their walls with colourful art installations, they keep things interesting by changing their décor every couple of months. Last year saw them scribble essay paragraphs and Manga characters onto their walls. If you're after a slice of Arkham Asylum, nip down to **Odd** (0161 833 0070). A moose's head, an Arabian boudoir and a range of disturbing photos make it look like it was decorated by a crazy man. If soft-core porn masquerading as art's your thing, then pop over to **Snook** in Fallowfield (0161 248 0546). You'll find photos of 'minimalist' clothing, a big screen projecting the latest in Swedish entertainment and a group of lads with their eyes popping out of their heads.

www.itchymanchester.co.uk

Drink

FALLOWFIELD PUBS

The Cheshire Cat
256 Wilmslow Road
(0161) 236 0012

A tumour growing on the side of the Queen of Hearts, this is the very worst of the Scream bars. Generally, Scream pubs are cheesy, tacky and a little grubby, but the irony of it all and the cheap drinks make them strangely fulfilling. Not so at Cheshire Cat, where you're just sitting on an uncomfortable seat in a crappy little bar being wound up by scallies, looked down on by power-tripping bouncers and asphyxiated by the lack of atmosphere. Stand up, leave, go to Trof. Never return.

◉ *Mon–Sat, 12pm–11pm;*
Sun, 12pm–10.30pm

Friendship Inn
353 Wilmslow Road
(0161) 224 5758

An oasis in the student wasteland of Fallowfield, the Friendship Inn provides refuge from the vodka-soaked culture of nearby bars. Standing unobtrusively on Wilmslow Road, this cavernous watering hole is a real treat if you like an old-fashioned pub. Enjoy a full range of well-priced real ales in a laid-back, friendly joint; sample the guest beer if you're feeling adventurous. Maybe take in a football match, safe in the knowledge that you won't be drenched in second-hand booze. Oh, and there's a pub quiz every Tuesday – so you can drink while you think.

◉ *Mon–Sat, 12pm–11pm;*
Sun, 12pm–10.30pm

Drink

The Orange Grove
304 Wilmslow Road
(0161) 224 1148

You might want to skip this review if you're not an undergrad, as the Orange Grove operates a student-only policy. As such, drinks are cheap – winos can buy two large glasses of Jacob's Creek and get the rest of the bottle free. Serious spirits drinkers can pick up a double and mixer for just £2.50. Despite lacking somewhat in atmosphere, there's plenty going on, with quiz night on Mondays and band night on Sundays. The Orange Grove is also the place to sup when the sun is shining, as there is plenty of outside seating on the terrace to perv on that fitty from your Shakespeare class.

Mon–Sat, 11am–2am;
Sun, 11am–12.30am

Robinskis
5–7 Wilbraham Road
(0161) 257 3736

A firm favourite with Fallowfield residents, 'Robbo's' is synonymous with excess. Think binge-drinking, bad dancing and vomiting, and you get the idea. This is the place for students to get wildly drunk, and maybe, just maybe, get lucky. The décor is bland, the bar understaffed, and the bouncers aren't too friendly either. That said, Robinski's is enormously popular. The perfect student combination of cheap drinks (vodka and Red Bull starts at £1 on Tuesday's 'vodbull night') and cheesy pop keeps the punters coming back for more. Don't forget your yellow card, and bear in mind that it's students only after 9pm.

Mon–Sun, 12pm–12am

www.itchymanchester.co.uk

Drink

NORTHERN QUARTER BARS

The Bay Horse
35 Thomas Street
(0161) 661 1041

With such devotion to tubes-of-glue-to-be, you'd expect to see a couple of neigh cows chowing down on hay in the corner. Sadly, the closest you're going to get are the framed photographs on the wall. The Bay Horse is Northern Quarter down to its very bones. Cool leather couches, an electric atmosphere and what we're going to charitably call a downstairs dungeon all mean you'd best not be expecting debauchery. Unless you want it with a horse, and we don't dig that whole Equus vibe.

Mon-Sat, 12pm-11pm;
Sun, 12pm-10.30pm

Common
39–41 Edge Street, Northern Quarter
(0161) 832 9245

Common has spent approximately sod all on décor and looks quite shabby. Normally, this wouldn't be a problem, but recently we've been worried about confusing it with the equally ugly and common Lilly Allen, and we'd hate to accidentally ask her for a drink. Proving that upholstery will always play second fiddle to atmosphere, it's always crammed (we promise that's the last Lilly Allen comparison). Ignore the occasional wannabe rock star (sunglasses at midnight, indoors? Honestly...) and head to the best post closing time drinking den in the area – in your trainers if you like.

Mon-Wed, 5pm-12am;
Thu-Sat, 5pm-2am

Bluu
Smithfield Market, Thomas Street
(0161) 839 7995

One of the coolest NQ venues; clientele look distinctly like they have jobs, cars, showers, etc. The expert staff manage to be smiley and attentive even when things get busy and they're pulling creamy pints faster than a dairy farmer. Soulful vibes and a neat terrace make these three floors more popular than a new lottery winner on a council estate, especially at weekends, so arrive early to avoid nippy queues and look forward to excellently high times perched atop teetering stools. It Bluu Itchy's socks clean off.

Sun-Mon, 12pm-12am; Tue-Thu,
12pm-1am; Fri-Sat, 12pm-2am; Food,
Mon-Sun, 12pm-6pm

Drink

Night & Day Café
26 Oldham Street
(0161) 236 4597

Often, when you sit in one of the many other Northern Quarter bars, you get the feeling it would rather be Night & Day. The staff, with their immaculate hair and co-ordinated outfits, would rather be at Night & Day, serving cans of Red Stripe rather than draught Staropramen. The walls would rather be covered in slightly tatty posters for gigs, the chairs would rather be slightly unstable and the toilets would rather be slightly less savoury. Night & Day is what all the other bars want to be like, on their knees in the night, saying prayers in the street light. Oh, and it's a serious gig venue too.
Mon–Sat, 11am–2am

Odd
30–32 Thomas Street
(0161) 833 0070

Shamefully, Odd isn't odd in the slightest. This aside, Odd is actually rather brilliant. So much so we're going to rename it. The Brilliant Bar That Lies No More is one of the Northern Quarter's best bars. The insides are a laid-back and trendy affair and you can't help but feel that this is where good drinkers go to die. Modern artwork adorns the walls, although those brave enough to venture into the basement 'pimp' area may need shades to avoid being blinded by the bling seating. The Brilliant Bar That Lies No More has lovely staff and lovely beer, and is the perfect place to get a drink.
Mon–Sat, 11am–11pm;
Sun, 11am–10.30pm

---

bluu

Smithfield Market Buildings
Northern Quarter
Manchester, M4 1BD
0161 8397195
Manchester@bluu.co.uk
www.bluu.co.uk

Stylish informal dining...retro kitsch surroundings...slinky drinks and creatively concocted cocktails...service second to none

•

Award winning...in the Northern Quarter, we don't do things by halves

•

Open 12pm 'til late through the week, and even later at weekends, with food served 12pm–10pm

•

Available for private hire

Drink

OXFORD ROAD BARS

The Cornerhouse
70 Oxford Street
(0161) 200 1508

This bar, restaurant, art gallery and cinema is many things to many people. Students may be able to spot lecturers drinking, chatting and generally not marking essays, which might explain the tremendously obscure Monday night quiz for those with in-depth knowledge of surrealism, German cinema and the 1980s cast of *Neighbours*.

- *Mon–Wed, 9.30am–11pm; Thu–Sat, 9.30am–12am; Sun, 11.30am–10.30pm; Food, Mon–Wed, 11am–11pm; Thu–Sat, 11am–12am; Sun, 11.30am–10.30pm*
- *Tuna melt, £5.25*
- *£11.50*

Kro2
Oxford House, Oxford Road
(0161) 236 1048

In the olden days, you didn't have pubs on campus, and what is now Kro Bar was the headquarters of the Temperance Society. Perhaps the Victorians had premonitions of pissed-up women roaming the town, dressed as nuns, with 'shag my sister' written on their habits. Anyway, the whole temperance thing never really caught on, and Kro Bar's difficult second single, Kro2, is every bit as boozy as the original.

- *Mon–Thu, 8.30am–12am; Fri, 8.30am–2am; Sat, 10.30am–2am; Sun, 10.30am–12am; Food, Mon–Fri, 8.30am–10.30pm; Sat–Sun, 10.30am–10pm*
- *Danish loin of pork, £9.95*
- *£10.50*

Font Bar
7–9 New Wakefield Street
(0161) 236 0944

Like their steak sarnie – so tasty that you might try and chat it up after you've had a few on a Friday night – Font Bar is never overdone. The attitude couldn't be more relaxed if it had a tranquilliser dart in its rump. Tunes are alternative and funky, including nights with a BYO record policy. Party hire is free, and the substantial cocktail list is virtually free too: they're just two of your chunky pound coins all day, every day. Always comfortably busy; when a bar's this great, with such tasty steak baguettes, there won't be any problems trying to fillet.

- *Mon–Sat, 12pm–1am; Sun, 12pm–1am*
- *Peppered steak sarnie, £3.95*
- *Legendary cocktails, all £2*

WEEKENDS AT

FONT BAR~
NEW WAKEFIELD STREET
JUST OFF OXFORD ROAD
OPPOSITE THE BBC

www.fontbar.com

fridays~

INDIE / ELECTRO / 60'S / 70'S

£2 cocktails all day everyday!

241 peroni till 10pm

saturdays~

FUNK / SOUL / HIP HOP / DISCO

Drink

Sandbar
120–122 Grosvenor Street
(0161) 273 3141

Don't be fooled by the name; the pub is not in fact made of sand, nor will you see any small children with spades here. What you will find, however, is a very good jukebox and a split-level mish-mash of different rooms and styles. Think Skegness beach without the industrial waste. Half of the bar exudes the familiar cosiness of your gran's house while the rest of the place sports an outside/inside, industrial look with plenty of nooks and crannies for quiet drinks. Older students, young professionals and academic types come together to discuss clever things like Meccano and the virtues of a proportional response.

☾ *Mon–Fri, 12pm–11pm; Sat, 2pm–11pm*

Sola
Contact Theatre, Oxford Road
(0161) 274 0606

If you're ever feeling drained, uninspired or generally lacklustre in the creative department, you can come and recharge your batteries in Sola. Housed inside the strangely shaped Contact building, it's probably the only bar that we can say inspired us without the catalyst of seven double whiskeys and that strange-coloured drink in a pint glass which always seems to be at your table when you arrive. If the bright décor doesn't get you in the mood to write eighty words of irrelevant musings then you can always rely on the £3 cocktails. We know we did.

☾ *Mon–Thu, 11am–12am;*
Fri–Sat, 11am–2am;

Games for a laugh

Pubs with games save us from ourselves. And more importantly they save us from dull people who won't shut the hell up. God bless games, we say. **The Orange Grove** in Fallowfield has a plethora of games available. A giant Connect 4 and Jenga ensure you can irritate the other patrons with the sound of your high-pitched, childlike whooping. Or, if you'd prefer your entertainment to be a tad more virtual, then head over to the **Sand Bar** – a widescreen game of Pro Evo Soccer is always available for those who'd like to prove their gaming prowess. Other virtual entertainment can be found in **Fab Café**. Pick up a lightgun, rue throwing 50p away and go all Jack Bauer on the hordes of the undead. But wait, you've run out of change. Damn it.

Drink

OXFORD ROAD PUBS

The Cavendish
44 Cavendish Street
(0161) 226 7600

Do you like pubs to point out that they are young and funky with colourful signs and lots of unnecessary punctuation??? Do you wet yourself at the thought of cheap doubles and Blue WKD??? Does the idea of a 'crazy quiz' get you and your 'mad' friends all excited??? If you answered 'yes' to any of the above then the Cavendish should be right up your street. A cheap and cheerful pub aimed at getting students and the odd local off their trolley on vodka shots, with a beer garden for those wacky summer nights!!!

Mon–Sun, 12pm–12am

The Rampant Lion
17 Anson Road
(0161) 248 0371

It's ginormous. And we know that's not a word, but the size of this boozer really merits that description. With its dark walls, rich green and red leather seating and striking gothic exterior, the place is frothing over with character, good music and indie flair. The bar prices are a little painful to the average student pocket, although the live music and fantastic surroundings go some way to compensating. The beer garden with its authentic (possibly) Roman ruins is one of Manchester's best outdoor summer spots, while inside there's enough space to swing a lion.

Mon–Thu, 12pm–1am; Fri–Sat, 12pm–2am; Sun, 12pm–12.30am

Hardy's Well
257 Wilmslow Road
(0161) 257 0450

Situated on the edge of the no-man's land between Rusholme and Fallowfield, this iconic pub is best known for the Lemn Sissay poem that adorns its exterior wall, which nobody can ever quite manage to read to the end when passing in traffic. With a pool table for the more 'athletic' punters and big screen live sports, this is a traditional pub if ever there was one, with excellent bar staff and a clientele of locals and more chilled-out-than-average students. The beer garden ain't the prettiest, but at least it gives drinkers the opportunity to finish reading that bloody poem.

Sun–Thu, 4pm–11pm; Fri–Sat, 5pm–12pm

The Thirsty Scholar
50 New Wakefield Street
(0161) 236 6071

If Bill Sykes and his dog hopped on board a Virgin Express and made their way to Manchester, they may well have ended up at The Thirsty Scholar. Not because its clientele are made up of cheeky, youthful, cockney convicts who just love to pick-a-pocket-or-two, but because its location on a cobbled side street neatly tucked away underneath a railway arch does have something of the Victorian underworld to it. A small, atmospheric pub where thirsty scholars and taxpayers alike come together to enjoy the best in new live music and dance their socks off at weekends to DJ sets.

Mon–Sun, 12pm–12am

www.itchymanchester.co.uk

Drink

WITHINGTON PUBS

The Drop Inn
393 Wilmslow Road
(0161) 286 1919

Sky Sports, two pool tables, ample space and £1.50 on selected bottles. That's the good news, but it's all downhill from there. Located in Studentsville between Withington and Fallowfield, on the main route in towards the university, the Drop Inn is the sort of place you spend the drinks tokens from your fresher's handbook and then, like that drunken fumble you had in fresher's week, look back on with a curious mix of embarrassment, shame and inexplicable nostalgia.

⏰ *Sun–Thu, 12pm–12am;*
Fri–Sat, 12pm–2.30am

The Old House at Home
70 Burton Road
(0161) 446 2315

The Old House used to be a decent boozer, but it sold its soul. We'd like to tell them that adding gaming machines, chalk-board menus and alcopops does not automatically attract students, but we'd be too late. It does a range of bland, homogenised pub grub, Sunday lunch and curry nights, but is no competition for its neighbouring pubs and restaurants. On the upside, it's cheap, friendly and has ample space and screens for showing the football. The Old House is a family pub, so expect little nippers on a Sunday asking you if you like Action Men.

⏰ *Mon–Thu, 11.30am–11pm; Fri–Sat,*
11.30am–12am; Sun, 12pm–11pm

Four in Hand
108 Palatine Road
(0161) 448 9397

A word of warning when going to the Four in Hand; don't expect the bar staff to see you waiting at the bar, be served with any speed, be served with a decent pint, or be served in a manner that is in any way friendly, courteous or hospitable. Right, we just had to get that out of our system, but moving on, what you can expect is a big lively pub, with cheap drinks and bog-standard, cheap-as-chips pub grub that'll fill you up when you're in need of a stodge fix. The place gets rammed on a Sunday, and has a good atmosphere when the football's on.

⏰ *Sun–Thu, 11am–11pm;*
Fri–Sat, 11am–12am

Stay regular

Illustration by Joly Braime

AIN'T NOTHIN' QUITE LIKE STEPPING INTO A BAR AND BEING GREETED AS ONE OF THEIR OWN. HERE'S ITCHY'S GUIDE TO BECOMING AS REGULAR AS CLOCKWORK SOMEWHERE NEW

1 Learn the name of the publican's partner/pet/mum – Take a couple of mates and stand at the bar within earshot of the publican and engage in the 'what would your porn name be?' game (combine your pet's name with your mum's maiden name). After a while, get the publican to join in, and make up some new variants designed to extract info about the names of spouses, dad, etc. Next time you walk in, you'll be able to greet them with a friendly, 'Alright Dave, how's Sandra doing?'

2 Have your own pint mug – Take a vessel and ask them to keep it behind the bar for you. Then whenever you walk in, you can sup your beverage in style. You may want to save this for the second visit.

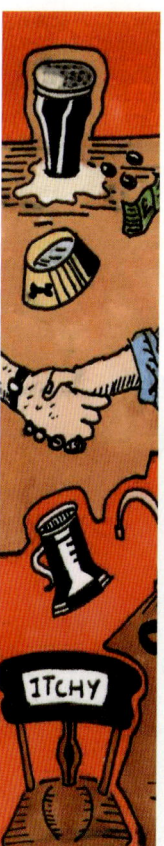

3 Know the pool rules – If they've already got a set of rules in place, learn what they are, loiter near the table and make sure you pounce upon any infraction to loudly proclaim 'That's not how we do things in here'. If there are no house rules, even better – make some up, don't tell anyone what they are, and then soon everyone'll need to ask you before playing.

4 Start a cribbage team – Unless the pub in question's populated by incontinent octogenarians, there's no chance that they'll have one. Get a 'Captain' T-shirt, and swan round asking randoms if they're ready for the big match. They'll have no idea what you're talking about, allowing you to explain your importance to the pub community.

5 Take a dog – Everyone loves a dog. Well, except asthmatics. But who cares about them? Those guys are already having enough of a wheeze.

IF YOU'RE AFTER GUILTY PLEASURES, WHY NOT GO FOR THE OLD CLASSICS? NO, NOT PROSTITUTION AND PICKING YOUR SCABS, BUT BRITNEY AND DALEKS

There's a Magna Carta sized list of reasons why you shouldn't go to **5th Avenue** (121 Princess Street, 0161 236 2754). It's packed with sweaty indie kids, the queue for the bar is atrocious and you need to be three pints under before you can even contemplate going. Yet strangely, we keep finding ourselves there. The same goes for Fallowfield's infamous **Queen of Hearts** (256 Wilmslow Road, 0161 249 0271). It's a nightclub in the same way you'd call a barn with a radio a music venue, but like small moths we are dazzled by its bright lights and attracted by the sounds of Britney and Kasabian.

Fab Café (111 Portland Street, 0161 236 2019) is our guilty finale. With trench coat and sunglasses on we slip into the geek-clique bar, praying we don't get recognised. It's a haven for nerds, but no self-respecting fashionista like us should be seen dead in there. Except we usually are. Why? They have a life-sized Dalek.

Guilty
pleasures

Illustration by Si Clark
www.si-clark.co.uk

Dance

Dance

CLUBS

42nd Street
2 Bootle Street
(0161) 831 7108

Do you like your clubs elegant and sophisticated, with a tuxedoed man tinkling away on a piano? Yes? Well if you see an entrance down a dingy alley with the words '42nd Street' above it, stay away. If however you like your nightclubs dark and dirty, with sweaty Debbie Harry, Julian Casablancas and Liam Gallagher look-alikes punching the air to indie rock 'n' roll classics until the early hours, then come on down. Get yourself a beer, roll your eyes as you think 'only in Manchester', and then join in.

Mon–Sun, 10pm–2am
Free–£4

Ampersand
Deansgate Court
(0161) 832 3038

Slicker than a greased up weasel, Ampersand is where all the cool kids go to swing their suave stuff. Once graced by the presence of P. Diddy and um, Mike 'ears taste yummy' Tyson (who apparently drank all the cosmopolitans in ten minutes), Ampersand is where it's all happening in Manchester. As you'd expect, this place is a treat to go to and soundly pummels the myth that you need to have a W1 postcode to run a classy club. It's a tad on the expensive side, but as you're sifting through bins for used tea bags, you can think back to the time when you lived like a millionaire.

Wed–Sat, 10pm–3am
Fri, £7; Sat, £10

5th Avenue
121 Princess Street
(0161) 236 2754

Swaggering drunkenly at the opposite end of the sophistication spectrum to its curiously chosen namesake, 5th Avenue is loud, cheap, sweaty and studenty. It's the kind of place where you'll find yourself at 2am, covered in beer and jumping up and down in a circle of strangers singing your heart out to *I am the Resurrection* which can only be a good thing. While indie music has flown in and out of fashion over the years, this archetypal indie discotheque has remained true, flying the guitar shaped flag high and providing plenty of stupidly cheap drinks to ease things along.

Mon–Thu, 10pm–2am; Fri–Sun, 10pm–3am
£1–£4

The Attic
59 New Wakefield Street
(0161) 236 6071

Far from being the resting place of old magazines, baby photos and sinister looking cobwebs, the Attic is a fine club perched on top of the finer Thirsty Scholar (although avoid the pubs next door – the plethora of leather-clad motorbikes might give you a clue about the customers). Back in the Attic, there's enough house and techno music to make even the keenest light stick waver start listening to Jack Johnson in protest. It's a bit of a pokey club and the toilets resemble the facilities on a coach, but don't worry about it. Your light sticks will glow just as hard. Glow little fella, glow.

Thu–Fri, 11pm–2am; Sat, 11pm–3am
£2–£5

Dance

BED
50 Sackville Street
(0161) 236 8300

'Booth' ain't a sexy word; it sounds like Chris Eubank talking about alcohol. Yet upholstered in leather next to kinky black mattresses in BED, a booth couldn't be slinkier if you coiled it into a spring and chucked it down a staircase. A classy yet laid back restaurant that showcases everything from live acoustic shows to karaoke, funk, and chocolate fountains, is Tribeca's downstairs hot spot BED an Itchy top pick? Do bears sheet in the woods?

Mon–Thu, 12pm–1am (Tue, 2am); Fri–Sat, 12pm–2.30am; Sun, 12pm–12.30am; Food, Mon–Sun, 12pm–9pm
Lamb shank, £9.95
Free

Club V
111 Deansgate
(0161) 834 9975

Despite rumours that Clubs I to IV were shut down by the unoriginal name organisation, Club V (officially known as Venus, but that would have totally ruined our intro) is a thumping club hidden away in Deansgate. Complete with a décor that wouldn't look out of place at one of Elton's bashes, Club V almost makes you forget that time you decided it would be a fun idea to go clubbing in Fallowfield. Almost. A drink costs a pretty penny, but what else were you going to spend that five pound note on anyway? What do you mean 'to buy an Itchy guide to Leeds?' Manchester all the way, baby.

Fri, 10.30pm–3am; Sat, 10.30pm–4am
£10

Jabez Clegg
2 Portsmouth Street
(0161) 272 8612

Buffy the Vampire Slayer should have been set in Manchester, if only because the sassy girl with the stick would have been useful for places like Jabez Clegg. Evil things come from here. Probably with tentacles. Having a girl with superpowers outside might have saved us from entering Manchester's hellmouth. But alas, no Buffy, meaning we were powerless as Jabez tempted us in with cheap beer, and now we have to pray that the photographic evidence of our visit doesn't turn up in 30 years to smear our campaign for presidency.

Mon–Fri, 11am–2am; Sat, 12pm–2am; Sun, 12pm–12.30am
£4–£5

www.itchymanchester.co.uk

Dance

Jilly's Rockworld
65a Oxford Street
(0161) 236 9971

Hardcore rockers have never really had a place to call home. You'll see them sitting in the corner of some indie club, complaining that the music isn't loud/angry/power-chordy enough. They look sad and unhappy. Jilly's Rockworld offers them a sanctuary – a place where they can listen to their favourite death metal tracks in the company of likeminded individuals. To make up for the years of hardships endured by the rawker community, they've made the club massive. With cheap beer. If you ever see an unhappy rocker, tell them to go here. They'll love you. And probably air guitar for your amusement.

Thu & Sat, 9pm–2am; Fri, 9pm–7am
Prices vary

Mint Lounge
46–50 Oldham Street
(0161) 228 1495

Cross *Moulin Rouge* with *Lost in Translation*, add a pinch of dirty disco and wrap it all up in a Cuban cigar, and you're some way to understanding the appeal of Mint Lounge. Originally touted as a burlesque club when it opened back in 2004, the feather boas and nipple tassles may have shimmied away but the Mint Lounge remains a decadent, seedy underground den for Manchester's alternative clubbing crowd. Intimate and charismatic, this is a sleazy, sexy and funky hybrid bar/club, with some of the city's best club nights plus live music events.

Thu, 8pm–2am; Fri–Sat, 10pm–4am;
Sun, 7pm–1am
Prices vary

M2
Peter Street
(0161) 839 1112

One of the few monster clubs left in Manchester – forget indie kids and their warbling idols, this is a club for Ibiza rep wannabes. Three floors of all your hip hop, dance and r 'n' b faves ensure that if you don't like a particular song you can probably nip downstairs and dance to something more to your taste. Wednesdays see the students pile in for the Athletic Union night, so if you enjoy people screaming 'TUUUUUNE' every 30 seconds, you'll have a whale of a time.

Wed–Thu, 10pm–2am;
Fri, 10pm–late; Sat, varies
Wed, £4 (students only);
Fri, free before 11pm/£5 after

Dance

The Music Box
65a Oxford Road
(0161) 273 5200

You can tell the Music Box is a fun sort of club. The atmosphere is bouncing and every punter looks like this is the best time they've had since Santa bought them a train set when they were five. No weird loners drinking whisky in the corner to be found here, just a big bunch of happy campers getting on with the important business of enjoying their night. Featuring the renowned Mr Scruff and Electric Chair nights, this underground dance club is one of the best places to pick up pointers for the light switch rave you're planning on hosting next month.

Wed-Thu, 8pm-12am;
Fri-Sat, 10pm-3am

One Central Street
1 Central Street
(0161) 211 9000

A very low-key, up-market New York-style basement club with a helpful name that corresponds exactly to its address. Genius. Thursdays are painfully beautiful and trendy, but the weekend sees a more relaxed and varied clientele, with very loud music covering house and funk with a twist of disco. Dance your socks off around the cast iron pillars or relax in one of the large leather clad booths – just don't expect to be able to hold an intelligible conversation with anyone unless you're proficient in sign language or telepathy. Smile, nod and get yourself another vodka tonic.

Thu, 9.30pm-3am; Fri-Sun, 10pm-3am
£4-£6

Ohm
28-34 High Street
(0161) 834 1392

Ohm caused a bit of a stir when it decided to advertise its new student lap dancing night by sending sparsely clad models a-flyering around Fallowfield. Shocked parents quickly regretted not sending their wide-eyed freshers somewhere a little quieter. Like Serbia. A classy little club, you'd expect Dita Von Teese to walk through the door at any second. We'd love to continue this review, but we get the feeling you only want to know when the lap dancing night is on. Wednesday. Sigh. People only want us for our superior knowledge of Manchester clubs.

Mon, 10pm-2am; Wed, 9pm-2am;
Sat, 10.30pm-4am; Sun, 6pm-12am

Dance

Paparazzi
2a The Printworks
(0161) 832 1234

Alas, no tabloid snappers waiting outside, but rather a snazzy club in the Printworks. Looking sexier than Angelina Jolie on a red carpet, Paparazzi is where you'll find the classier clientele of the Printworks. Except on Thursdays. The Airport night is when the students decide to wash their clothes and take the bus ride to town. Friday and Saturday are the nights of sophistication – well, as sophisticated as 2 for 1 on alcopops and vomit stains on dresses can be. Roll with it and take a packet of clean up wipes.

Mon–Tue, 9pm–2am; Wed, 10pm–2.30am; Thu & Sun 9pm–2.30am; Fri, 10pm–3am; Sat, 10pm–4am
Prices vary

The Phoenix
Precinct Centre, Oxford Road
(0161) 272 5921

The Phoenix used to be regarded as one of the best club venues around. However, like Christian Slater's film career, it's suffered from a little dip in form of late. Having seen its best club night, Tangled, jump ship in favour of the students' union basement, the Phoenix is somewhat of a clipped bird. It's still a phenomenal venue, but you can't help but feel that the loss of such a major club has been a bit of a kick in the delicates for all concerned. Will the phoenix rise from the flames? Will we ever stop using clichés? Only time will tell.

Mon–Fri, 11.30am–11pm; Fri–Sat, 6pm–4am; Sun, 6pm–10.30pm
Prices vary

Dance

Po Na Na
42 Charles Street
(0161) 272 6044

Ok, so you're a Morroccan sultan and you've just arrived in Manchester on your camel. Where do you go? Why, Po Na Na of course (obviously only once you've cleared things with the immigration officers). You may struggle to get your mount down the stairs, but you'll feel right at home in this intimate, North-African inspired night spot. With its low arched ceilings, and softly lit and well-cushioned cubby holes it could easily be mistaken for a luxurious sultan's harem, if it weren't for the DJ booth and great cocktail list.

Tue–Thu, 8pm–2am;
Fri–Sat, 8pm–3am
Free–£5

The Roadhouse
8–10 Newton Street, Piccadilly
(0161) 237 9789

It's grimy. It looks sinister. You'll probably get sneered at. All hail the beauty of the Roadhouse – a hardcore indie venue for those tired of seeing the dance floor fill up every time a DJ plays Snow Patrol. This is no syrupy 5th Avenue experience and there's not a bewildered looking fresher in sight. The clientele know their music and if they don't, they're going to buy it on vinyl tomorrow morning. Although if you'd like to save your cash, go and listen to the music in the kebab shop below. If you've never tried a reverberating pizza, you've never lived.

Mon–Thu, 8pm–1am; Fri, 8pm–3am;
Sat, 10pm–3am; Sun, 8pm–12am
£3–£8

The Queen of Hearts
256 Wilmslow Road
(0161) 257 2119

Theoretically, the very premise of a queue is a good one. Exciting things normally precede the start of a queue – there could be muffins or an autographed photo of David Hasselhoff. In an effort to ruin our idealistic opinions on queues, the Queen of Hearts employs a strict policy of making people stand in the rain. If you want a crowded Scream bar with intoxicated students 'dancing', queue here. If you want to check out the footballer's wives dancing around handbags, queue here. If you want to wage war with the rugby-shirt wearing clientele, queue here. If you want muffins, try Tesco.

Mon–Thu, 12pm–11pm; Fri–Sat,
12pm–2am; Sun, 12pm–10.30pm

www.itchymanchester.co.uk

Dance

Sankey's
Radium Street
(0161) 950 4201

Sankey's is shut. No, it's open again. No, wait, it's closed down. Err, it's open once more. Like an episode of an Australian soap opera, Sankey's has kept us in a state of constant confusion regarding its health. Tired of the rumours, we kidnapped the manager and after making him listen to Radiohead for ten hours, finally got the truth: Sankey's, Manchester's finest club venue, is open once again. Except in a different venue. Still, expect the same high quality club nights, the same expensive bottles of water and the same aching limbs after dancing for six hours.

Thu–Fri, 10pm–3am; Sat, 10pm–4am
Members, £10; Non-members, £12

South
4a South King Street
(0161) 831 7756

If you're heading to South, you may want to tuck an A-Z in your handbag – it's a cheeky little rascal to find, this one. Those of you who pass the unofficial wilderness ranger's test will find yourself in a nifty little underground club. Populated by indie kids, retro kids (so over 30s then) and drank-too-much-beer kids, South offers a mix of classic indie and old skool tunes and bottles of water to satisfy the wide selection of clientele. It's not the prettiest bar to look at, but then we think Christian Bale isn't that much of a looker. Complaints to the usual address.

Fri–Sat, 10pm–3am
Fri £4–£5.50; Sat, £6–£7

Satan's Hollow
101 Princess Street
(0161) 236 0666

Satan's Hollow is a place of sin. With a giant effigy of the dark lord (Satan, not Donald Rumsfeld) overseeing the shenanigans of the damned, this club is full of the most alternative members of society. And despite the consequences of eternal damnation, it's also a very fun place to hang out. Erring away from the hardest of hardcore and sticking to real, damned cheese at the weekends, we'd advise you to stay away from the dark corners – they're a veritable hotspot for the nefarious deeds of amorous youths, and no one needs to be reminded what it looks like when teenagers get frisky.

Mon–Tue, 10.30pm–3am; Thu, 10.30pm–4am; Fri–Sat, 9pm–3am

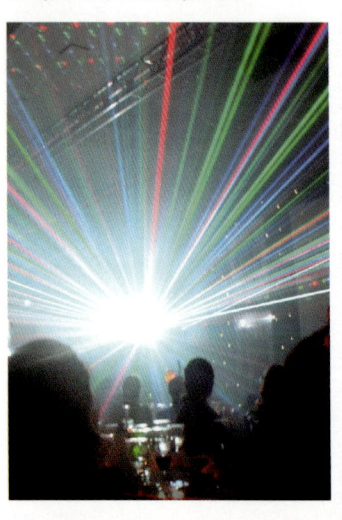

Safe and sound

Illustration by Thomas Denbigh

THE DANCE-FLOOR IS A SCARY REALM. IF YOU WANT TO MAKE IT OUT ALIVE, YOU'LL NEED SOME INSIDER KNOWLEDGE, SO GRAB PITH HELMET AND GLO-STICKS AND FOLLOW ITCHY ON A DISCO SAFARI

HEN PARTIES
Distinguishing features: Normally perform their all-female pre-mating ritual in a circular dance around sequined receptacles containing grooming apparel. The leader usually wears a letter L and some kind of sexual apparatus on her head.
Survival: For males under 60, camouflage is the best bet. Itchy recommends a bright pink mini-skirt, padded boob tube and red lippy.

HOMO NARCOTICUS
Distinguishing features: This unusual subspecies is mesmerised by repetitive rhythms and flashing lights, and has a peculiar ability to move all limbs and appendages at once in contrary directions, including eyes and ears.
Survival: These malcos are guaranteed to spill your drink on themselves. Put your bev in a bike bottle or go the whole way and throw a sacrificial pint at them before you start dancing.

THE LADS
Distinguishing features: Alpha males indulging in competitive play, such as mixing several beverages in the same glass, and then drinking the whole lot as quickly as possible.
Survival: A propensity to punch the air during power ballads can lead to injury among taller adventurers. Itchy suggests you don a helmet and hit the deck if you hear the line 'Oooh baby do you know what that's worth?'.

UNDERAGE DRINKERS
Distinguishing features: Identified by greasy hair, pale skin and vacant eyes, this genus often regurgitate upon themselves, presenting a hazard to bystanders. Females are impervious to cold and wear very little.
Survival: Enlist their natural predators – larger and more primitive hominids called bouncers, who covet the hair of the underage drinkers, being themselves a furless species.

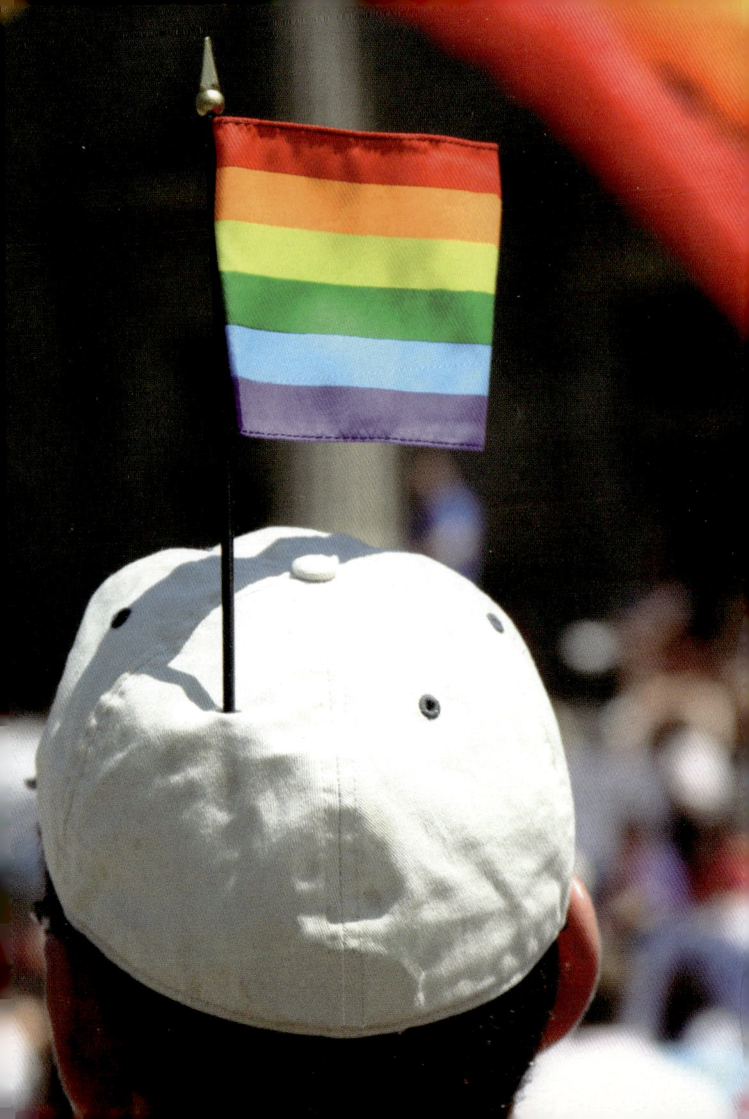

Gay

Gay

BARS

AXM
10 Canal Street
(0161) 236 6005

If there is a gay elite, then surely they all go to AXM. Famed for its high class, this place is only for the sophisticated and seriously sexy. Much like ourselves. Serving the suits-and-cash side of Manchester's gay scene, AXM has got a bit of a mixed vibe. Is it a bar, an internet café, a cocktail lounge, or everything all mushed together? Only you can decide, but whatever you do, don't come here in anything other than the best labels and finest cuts. You wouldn't want to embarrass yourself now would you?

🕐 *Mon–Thu, 12pm–1am;*
Fri–Sat, 12pm–2am; Sun, 12pm–12.30am

Taurus
1 Canal St
(0161) 236 4593

Taurus seems to be quite comfortable within its role as the place for the more mature gay crowd, and as a result it's taken a wholly grown-up and classy approach to dining and boozing. Currently seeing a wave of celebrations for civil ceremonies, this is the place to be if you need your faith in good old-fashioned love restored. Not to say it's boring mind. These guys have still got a whole lot of naughty fun left in their boots, but they know how to do it in style. A true treat, Taurus is the bull's bits.

🕐 *Mon–Thu, 12pm–11pm; Fri–Sat, 12pm–1am; Sun, 12pm–10.30pm; Food, Mon–Sat, 12pm–10pm; Sun, 12pm–9.30pm*
💰 *£10.75*

Eden Bar
3 Brazil Street
(0161) 237 9852

When you've got a canal at your disposal you have to be nice to it. They get lonely, you know, with only the shopping trolleys to talk to. If you're interested in spending some quality time with the local waterways, then pop along here and lounge on the barge. It's really quite a jolly place to get some decent food and drinks, and if it rains (rain? Manchester? Never.) then the inside is cosy and inviting. Swashbuckling like a pirate is strictly forbidden though. Shame that.

🕐 *Mon–Wed, 11am–12am; Thu–Sat, 11am–2am; Sun, 11pm–12am;*
Food, Mon–Sun, 11am–9pm
🍴 *Thai red curry, £8.95*
💰 *£5.50*

Olive Delicatessen
Regency House, 36–38 Whitworth Street
(0161) 236 2360

All-hours gourmet food and booze; way better than M&S, maybe even better than S&M. Eat, drink, and get merrier than Christmas; they serve 40 gourmet vodkas and coffee so good you'd accept it even if the offer came from the Elephant Man, so shoot to kill, then wake yourself back up with an espresso. Their hazelnut caramel Lumpy Bumpy cake is incredible, and there are condoms for sale at the counter if all the sensuousness inspires you to pop home for a bit of rhyming rumpy pumpy. We certainly know which we prefer the taste of.

🕐 *Mon–Fri, 8am–10pm;*
Sat–Sun, 9am–10pm
🍴 *BLT, £2.70*

Gay

Velvet

2 Canal Street
(0161) 236 9003

Velvet is as sumptuous as the name suggests. Lose yourself in a big fat comfy chair and imagine your legions of adoring fans waiting for you outside, clamouring to be near you, just to tell their grandchildren that they touched you. The food is top banana (they don't actually sell bananas, but if they did they'd probably be the best bananas in town) and the cocktails show the touch of an expert. Avoid if you're scared of goldfish.

Mon–Thu, 11am–12pm; Fri–Sat, 11am–2am; Sun, 11am–10pm;
Food, Mon–Sun, 11am–10pm
Moroccan lamb, £8.95
£7.95

Essential Nightclub

Bloom Street
(0161) 236 0077

Looking for some hot stuff this evening, baby? If you want a feast of man flesh then get yourself to Essential, the unabashed and totally decadent gay clubbing capital of Manchester. Always up for a laugh, always ready to party and always in the campest possible taste, Essential offers a truly naughty night out. They do have a majority gay and lesbian door policy, but don't seem too strict on enforcing it. Be warned though, hen parties are a big no dice. Never mind though, at least you can shake your booty without the fear of getting hit by a flying hair band covered in flashing willies.

Thu, 11pm–4am; Fri, 11pm–5am; Sat, 11pm–7am; Sun, 11pm–4am

CLUBS

Club Alter Ego

105–107 Princess Street
(0161) 236 9266

Dearly beloved, we are gathered here today to mourn the loss of Mutz Nutz, the liveliest and grimiest house and cheese venue the Village had to offer. It served us well in the small hours of the morning and we loved it dearly. Fear not though, for out of this terrible, sombre affair will rise the dawning of a new, cleaner, refurbished era, and it shall be known as Alter Ego and it shall be glorious in all its finery and debauched secrets. Don't cry, for Poptastic still reigns supreme. Peace be with you all. Amen.

Tue, 11pm–3.30am; Fri, 11pm–4am; Sat, 11pm–5am

www.itchymanchester.co.uk

Gay

Manto
46 Canal Street
(0161) 236 2667

Got a hot date? Wanna take your special someone dancing 'till the wee small hours of the morning? Well then, take your man to Manto (hell's bells, Itchy's on comic form). After a refurb and a reconsideration of their dress code, it's been a long time since Manto was the place where your feet stick to the carpets. It's gone all wipe-clean and slinky, and it is definitely one of the best places to go dancing on Canal Street. With a completely mixed-bag crowd and music range, there really is something for even the fussiest reveller, but leave it 'til after midnight; it's the kind of place to end up in, not start out at.

Mon–Thu, 11am–2am; Fri, 11am–3am; Sat, 11am–4am; Sun, 12pm–2am

Via Fossa
28–30 Canal Street
(0161) 236 6523

Sprawled over what seems to be about five million floors, this place is a goldmine of quirky furniture and a veritable Tardis of hidden corners, perfect for the secret smoocher in you. For those of you who like your fun in larger groups (no funny business mind), there are massive long banquet tables and thrones for you to lounge around while you drink shots and cocktails at bargain prices. The crowd's fun and totally random, as is the music, and there is nothing better than supping your G&T on a throne. We like much.

Mon–Thu, 11am–1.30am; Fri, 11am–2.30am; Sat, 11am–3.30am; Sun, 12pm–1.30am; Food, Mon–Sun, 12pm–10pm
£7

New Union
111 Princess Street
(0161) 228 1492

Sometimes you have to learn from your own mistakes. Like the time when we were told not to stick our tongue in a plug socket but did it anyway, or when we thought it'd be a good idea to make a special cocktail using every bottle in our drinks cabinet. Itchy believes in letting you make your own mistakes, but if it was up to us, and we ruled the world, then we'd tell you to go somewhere other than this. There's nothing wrong with it per se, but it just doesn't have the atmosphere of some of its Canal Street cousins. But you're free to make your own decisions; you're all big boys now. Sort of.

Mon–Sat, 11am–2am; Sun, 12pm–12.30am

SHOPS

Clone Zone
36–38 Sackville Street
(0161) 236 1398

There are few venues in Manchester where you can buy birthday cards, sex toys and dressing up gear at the same checkout. And even better, there's not a sleazy chain curtain in sight as you peruse the stock in Clone Zone. They sell everything a person needs to keep their sex life ticking over and there are enough toys and trinkets to make even Pete Burns blush, but it's all in the best possible taste. It certainly opened Itchy's eyes, even if we did get a bit giggly around the fetish wear.

Mon–Thu, 11am–10pm; Fri–Sat, 11am–11pm; Sun, 12pm–7pm

SO YOU'RE A FRIEND OF DOROTHY WHO'S FOUND THEMSELVES IN A NEW TOWN, AND IT MIGHT AS WELL BE THE EMERALD CITY, YOU'RE SO CLUELESSLY GREEN. HOW DO YOU TRACK DOWN THE BEST PINK PLACES? LET ITCHY GUIDE YOUR RUBY SHOES WITH SOME PEARLS OF WISDOM…

Gay abandoned

There's no place like homo – Just because you're out of the closet doesn't necessarily mean that you love the great outdoors; camping it up isn't for everyone. However, the most kitsch, flamboyant venues are generally well advertised and typically the easiest ones to find; their mass appeal means you usually get a fair old proportion of straights in there too, enjoying their recommended weekly allowance of cheese, but you should have no trouble tracking down a few native chatty scenesters.

Even if their tastes aren't quite yours, they can give you the lowdown on the more subtle gay haunts, and you and Toto will be going loco in no time.

Scally or pally? – Various gay fetishes for chav-style fashions can make it hard to tell a friendly bear pit from a threatening lions' den full of scallies, especially if you've only heard rumours that somewhere is a non-hetters' hot spot. Be cautious in places packed with trackies unless you want your Adid-ass kicked.

Get board – Internet message boards have honest, frequently updated tips; magazines like *Diva* and *Gay Times* have links to local forums on their sites. Click your mouse, not your heels, and get ready to go on a bender.

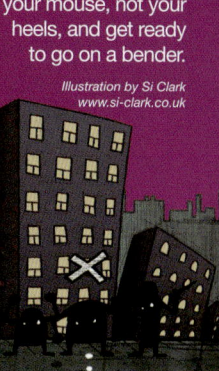

Illustration by Si Clark
www.si-clark.co.uk

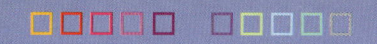

Shop

Shop

AREAS

Deansgate

Home to the rich and nearly famous, you'll see many a confused student walking the gold paved paths of Deansgate (they heard Armani had a sale on – those student loans aren't going to spend themselves, after all). This is the classy quarter of Manchester and many of the more exclusive brands call this their home. Here you'll find silk ties from Armani, a six-button wool and silk suit from Kendal and many a prospective Patrick Bateman perusing them all (in terms of corporate agenda, rather than murderous habits, we hope). It's also got quite a few classy restaurants so you can show off those new French cufflinks to your yuppie brethren.

Market Street

Had George Lucas made the brave and daring decision to set *Star Wars* on Market Street instead of the planet of Tatooine, the fate of the galaxy would've been significantly different. Luke Skywalker, unable to resist the charms of the Arndale centre, would have spent the first three films shopping. The cliff-hanger of *The Empire Strikes Back* would have been him losing his credit card. Han Solo would have spent all day drinking venti lattes in Starbucks and Princess Leia would have been last seen in Primark. Indeed, the only notable set pieces of the film would have been Obi-Wan's lightsabre battle with a couple of scallies and Luke's daring attempt to get to Music Zone before it closed for the evening.

Shop

The Triangle Shopping Centre
(0161) 834 8961

90% of brands within this slick tri-umph of design can't be found anywhere else in Manc or the North West, so if you've an ounce of style you won't dodge 'em. Forget high street duds with the life expectancy of a fairground goldfish; choose designer creations from Unique Boutique, JOY and Vicky Martin. Sort out your smalls at Calvin Klein underwear, large it with hand-crafted bling from Christopher James, and get trainers and training from Up & Running. Not that you'll need any help in the human race, mind; you're obviously winning already, you superior being, you.

Mon–Wed, 10am–6pm; Thu–Sat, 10am–7pm; Sun, 11am–5pm

Selfridges in the City
1 Exchange Square
(0161) 838 0706

A reason to keep on buying scratch cards and invest in pyramid schemes, Selfridges is a treat for those willing to splash the cash. Fashionable clothing for men and women, a top shoe selection and a beauty parlour are available all under one roof. The 'design your own T-shirt' area is truly something special – doodling has never been so much fun. There's also a lingerie section for those willing to gawp and wish they could convince their partners to wear them. And for those who also enjoy wearing underwear, too. But the gawpers are our fave thing about the place.

Mon–Fri, 10am–8pm; Sat, 9am–8pm; Sun, 11am–5pm

DEPARTMENT STORES

Harvey Nichols
Exchange Square
(0161) 828 8888

If you're married to a 73-year-old oil baron or just robbed HSBC, then you should find your way to Harvey Nichols. This three-tier department store is the epicentre of Manchester fashion. Shoes, clothes and food for those with overly-large wallets, sacks of gold or doting partners are all here. A bar, beauty zone and extensive accessories section mean that it's like drugs for fashion junkies. Don't take drugs though readers – you'd have to spend that hard earned inheritance on bail money, instead.

Mon–Wed & Fri, 10am–7pm; Thu, 10am–8pm; Sat, 9am–7pm; Sun, 12pm–6pm

www.itchymanchester.co.uk

Shop

MEN'S CLOTHING

Bluu
31 Market Street
(0161) 832 3866

Those of you worried that a defunct boy band will profit from your excursion to this fashionable menswear store needn't fear. Bluu is the hipper older brother of Manchester's mainstream clothes stores. Tailored wear for everything the modern major man could ever need to impress their girlfriend's parents, this is casual clothing without the shorts and sandals with socks. It's not too pricey, so you should have no excuses for dressing like your grandparents. Although we hold onto the hope that knotted handkerchiefs will make a comeback one day.

Mon–Sat, 7am–8pm; Sun, 11am–5pm

Oi Polloi
70 Tib Street
(0161) 831 7870/831 7781

Sadly, some ruffian/student has stolen the Magpie Road sign from outside this trendy store. Still, Oi Polloi remains one of the best places to pick up unique and cool threads for your wardrobe. Outdoor brands and footwear are particularly snazzy in this hidden away store and you'd be forgiven for coming out with bags full of clothing. If you want to escape judgement, tell any acquaintances you bump into that they're your girlfriend's. That, or carry a baseball bat. No one will dare look at you funny. Except maybe the police. But with the rest of your fashionista garb on you, you could maybe claim it's a fashion accessory. Or run.

Mon–Sat, 10am–6pm

Cast
49–51 Thomas Street
(0161) 832 5100

A Northern Quarter landmark, you can locate Cast through the sound of skater kids rollerblading on the in-store half pipe. Yes, this is truly home for the fashion-conscious skater. Specialising in clothing that's probably not aerodynamic, Cast ensures you can try to emulate Tony Hawk's moves and look cool at the same time. It's a nice enough shop for those that enjoy watching sports of the extreme variety, and at least they can console themselves with the fact that they look fashionable while en route to A & E with a broken leg. Don't worry if you hear screams coming from the ambulance either. They probably just had to cut open the trousers.

Mon–Sat, 10am–6pm; Sun, 12pm-4pm

Shop

UNISEX CLOTHING

Pop Boutique
34–36 Oldham Street
(0161) 237 9688

This shop is like stepping into your grandma's wardrobe back when she was trendy. Even the smell is the same. Mmm, mothballs. Home to never-ending rails of colourful retro gear, Pop Boutique sell their own range of 'Pop' retro T-shirts, jeans and cords. Quirky décor like lamps from the 60s accompany your shopping experience, and have you seriously wondering whether you have actually stumbled into a time portal. If it's really dark though, you've probably walked into your nan's closet. You can tell by the actual mothballs.

Mon–Sat, 10am–6pm; Sun, 11am–5pm

Urban Outfitters
Market Street
(0161) 817 6640

Calm down Akala fans. This isn't somewhere you're going to be able to kit yourself out in the styles of all the anaemic versions of hip-hop and r 'n' b that make up UK urban music (seriously, any decent UK street music always gets referred to by a different term, presumably meaning that 'urban' is used as another way of saying 'shit'). What this actually is, is a three-floor paradise of hip and trendy clothing. As a result, it's the shop of choice for the trendsetters from the North.

Mon–Wed & Fri–Sat, 10am–7pm;
Thu, 10am–8pm; Sun, 11am–6pm

Pumpkins
319 Wilmslow Road
(0161) 248 0908

When your Topshop collection of T-shirts and summer dresses just won't cut it, Pumpkins serves up the Bond-esque goods. Like a fun version of a library, this Fallowfield store rents out a collection of dapper tuxedos and shiny ball gowns for those once in a lifetime moments. Of course if you throw up over your jacket or dress, then no matter what outfit you plumped for, you're still going to look like a muppet on the photographs. But your face probably won't look as amusing as those of the people who have to share the vomit-reeking air with you. Still probably best not to vom though.

Mon–Sat, 10am–6pm

Westworld
The Triangle, Exchange Square
(0161) 832 0070

Penguins are fun. They waddle. They dress like they're serving entrées at a dinner party. They're our second favourite animal after scallies. However, penguins could be cooler. They could shop at Westworld. Casual clothing for men and women, this is a breath of fresh, Antarctic air, away from the stuffy, clichéd gear of the high street. Stocking cool jeans, T-shirts and hoodies, the only problem is that it's pricey. Which is probably why penguins don't shop here.

Mon–Wed, 9.30am–6pm;
Thu–Sat, 9.30am–7pm

Unique Brands at Triangle Shopping Centre — triangle Shopping Centre

www.itchymanchester.co.uk

Shop

WOMEN'S CLOTHING

Jazz
105 Beech Road, Chorlton
(0161) 881 0721

Nestled in the warm suburban bosom of Chorlton, Jazz is well worth the bus ride/car journey/donkey hitching required to travel there. Offering casual clothing for the trendy urbanite, Jazz showcases local northern brands you'll happily sport among the most dedicated of fashionistas. More distinctive than a pair of laddered tights, the clothing is far better than the ridiculous store name, and you're likely to find some right fashion gems down here. Don't thank us. The squeal of delight as you find that killer top is reward enough.
Mon–Sat, 10am–6pm; Sun, 11am–5.30pm

Reiss
Trafford Centre
(0161) 746 8700

Fashionable clothing Trinny and Susannah wouldn't mind being seen out in, Reiss is the pinnacle of fashionable high street stores. And you can tell by the prices. If your wardrobe is beginning to look like your mum's then Reiss can rescue your self confidence with its sexy and downright fashionable clothing. Indeed, if you fancy a payday splurge, this should be your first port of call. Go on. Your pay cheque would be disappointed if you didn't.
Mon–Fri, 10am–10pm;
Sat, 10am–8pm; Sun, 12pm–6pm

Rags 2 Bitches
60 Tib Street
(0161) 835 9265

Decorated like the inside of a whore's boudoir (or erm, so we'd imagine – we're as pure as the driven snow at Itchy, don'tcher know) Rags to Bitches is as bold in its clothing as its name suggests. More upmarket than the neighbouring vintage chic havens, this year-old addition to the Northern Quarter provides its clientele with classy and luxurious clothing which doesn't look like it's already been worn for 40 years (think Affleck's Palace minus the mustiness). As well as fancy clobber, there's delectable handmade jewellery too tempting to leave in the shop. Well, too tempting for us, at least.
Mon–Sat, 11am–6pm

Unique Brands at Triangle Shopping Centre — triangle Shopping Centre

Shop

SHOES

Jake Shoes
28 King Street
(0161) 834 4326

Scene 2. Living Room. Judy, 21, enters. Her mum is reading the paper. Judy: 'Mum can I get new shoes?' Mum: 'What's wrong with your shoes?' Judy (sheepishly): 'Nothing. I just want new ones.' Mum: 'Where from?' Judy: 'Jake.' Mum: 'Is that your new boyfriend? Is he behind this? Don't do it. I did what your father wanted and now I've got three kids.' Judy: 'No it's an independent shoe store.' Mum: 'With a lot of fashionable yet affordable shoes?' [Judy nods]. Mum (sighs): 'Fine. But never let your boyfriend replace your birth control pills with Tic Tacs.'

Mon-Sat, 9.30am–5.45pm; Sun, 11am–5pm

Schuh
44–46 Market Street
(0161) 834 6521

A library of shoes plonked in the middle of Market Street. If you like your trainers to keep up with current trends, you really should burn the plastic here. Friendly staff and comfy seats make the Saturday crowd a little less irritating though you can't help but feel that the shoes would be more comfortable in a larger shop. Free range shoes are happier shoes. Regardless, a quick phone call to the riot police and a couple of cans of tear gas should clear the place out pretty quickly, allowing you to peruse with your preferred three metres of personal space.

Mon-Wed & Sat, 9am–7pm; Thu-Fri, 9am–8pm; Sun, 9am–4pm

Ran
7–8 St Ann's Arcade, off St Ann's Square
(0161) 832 9650

Feet should be covered. Feet look horrible and they smell funny (we assume you agree unless you're of 'speciality' interests, but then we're not talking to you, pervaloids). Praises be to the inventor of the shoe then. A foot sheath, protecting us all from the innate freakiness of our bipedal curse. Ran is one of these foot sheath places. It's also quite fashionable – turning the ugly foot into something of beauty, something to be admired. Not only is it a whitewash for the evolutionary throwbacks that are toes, but it also benefits from being an independent store – there's no one else with a Ran-dom selection of foot sheaths quite like theirs.

Mon-Sat, 9.30am–6pm; Sun, 11am–5pm

www.itchymanchester.co.uk

Shop

SECONDHAND

Oxfam Originals
11 Smithfield Buildings Oldham Street
(0161) 839 3160

While we all enjoy a good old root around a secondhand shop, Oxfam Originals does the hard job of finding all the elite clobber for you. The best of the best gear gets sent up to sunny Manchester and here you'll find the cream of secondhand donations. Vintage and retro stuff often finds its way up to these parts, and you'll need to be on the ball as the stuff flies off the shelves. Thankfully, deliveries every day ensure that even if you missed out on those 70s flares, there might be another pair tomorrow.
Mon–Sat, 10am–6pm; Sun, 12pm–5pm

St Ann's Hospice Furniture Shop
128 Mauldeth Road, Ladybarn
(0161) 445 7990

Those who can resist the siren call of mass-produced Swedish tables should head up to St Ann's Furniture Shop. A collection of excellent quality furniture, this shop is a godsend to the malnourished wallet of a student. Stocking a range of items from bedside tables to shelves, this truly is a relief for those who bought far too many clothes/DVDs/oddly shaped trinkets to university. Indeed, its location slap bang in the middle of Withington means you can probably lug your purchases back to your student accommodation without even breaking into a sweat.
Mon–Sat, 9.30am–4pm

Speak easy

ITCHY'S HELPFUL GUIDE TO INTERPRETING EXACTLY WHAT THOSE LOCALS ARE ON ABOUT...

'So how do I get to the Northern Quarter?'
I've bought a new scarf and suede blazer and need a mildly pretentious bar to wear them in without fear of recriminations.

'Monsoon season's finally over.'
Tomorrow it will rain.

'Fancy a trip to shanty town?'
Does anyone want to go and find some students to irritate in Fallowfield?

'Lets go grab ourselves a Manchester salad.'
I want some takeaway chips.

'Anyone want to go clubbing in St. Peter's Street?'
Let's go and wait in a queue for an hour and a half. For funsies.

Shop

BOOKS

Blackwells
University Precinct Centre
(0161) 274 3331

1pm – We have arrived in Manchester. Our guide led us slowly up Oxford Road and we set up camp sometime around midnight. Around noon, we reached Blackwells bookstore. Few people have witnessed the annual 'students rush to buy text books before their exams start' migration, and we're honoured that we should be a part of this exquisite event. 5pm – We have barred the gates, but cannot hold them for long. The ground shakes. Drums, drums in the deep. We cannot get out. A shadow moves in the dark. We cannot get out... they are coming.

Mon–Fri, 9am–7pm; Sat, 9am–5pm

Stanfords
39 Spring Gardens
(0161) 831 0250

Come, weary traveller, prepare for a journey 'cross land and sea, where you shall see giants walk and the lion roar. Stock up on maps here and journey well, friend.

Mon, Wed–Sat, 9am–6pm;
Tue, 9.30am–6pm

Borders
51 Regent Crescent, Trafford Centre
(0161) 202 9908

Paperchase, books, pencil-top erasers, Top Trumps, CDs, calendars. What a store.

Mon–Sat, 10am–10pm; Sun, 12pm–6pm

Oxfam Bookshop
605 Wilbraham Road, Chorlton
(0161) 881 7808

Time was, long ago, you'd walk into Oxfam and expect the book section to be populated with Mills and Boon novels. These novels of love, romance and thinly veiled metaphors for genitalia, were quite frankly a bit naff, so it's with a happy heart we reveal to you what was the very first Oxfam bookstore in the country. With different sections for kids, adults, education, classics and factual, there's a book for every occasion. Of course if you'd like to lie in the bath and dream of François the manly French pirate, the proudly-surviving romance section will happily tend to your every need.

Mon–Sat, 10am–5.30pm; Sun, 11am–4pm

Waterstone's
91 Deansgate
(0161) 832 1992

There's something about a shop that has more than one floor that just screams 'quality'. You don't see many Woolworths with a floor-guide and an elevator now, do you?

Mon–Fri, 9am–8pm; Sat, 9am–7pm;
Sun, 11am–5pm

WH Smith Trafford Centre
34 Peel Avenue
(0161) 755 0299

Sweets, books, pencils and cards. Bonza.

Mon–Fri, 10am–10pm; Sat, 10am–8pm;
Sun, 11.30am–6pm

Unique Brands at Triangle Shopping Centre

Shop

MUSIC

Fopp
19 Brown Street
(0161) 827 1620

A side street away from the behemoth of HMV, Fopp is blessed with two essential qualities that makes it a great music shop. 1) It has a funny name. 2) It has a staggeringly large collection of cheap music and DVDs. Both of these points mean that Fopp is an essential part of a Saturday wander around town. Fopp also stocks vinyl and is blessed with a coffee shop, for when the trials of carrying around your partner's shopping becomes too much, so you need a sit down and a biscuit.

☏ *Mon–Wed & Fri, 9am–6pm;*
Thu, 9am–7pm; Sun, 11am–5pm

Vinyl Exchange
18 Oldham Street
(0161) 228 1122

You either have to be quite poor or a complete skinflint to recycle tea bags. Thankfully, the same doesn't apply to records, so you can hand over mere pennies for Vinyl Exchange's secondhand record collection with your head held high. Pre-owned stock ranging from alternative dance to heavy metal means you can pick up your musical desires at half the price. They also have a grandiose collection of DVDs and vinyl (duh) downstairs so you need not limit your budget-saving techniques to Britney's back collection. Snigger.

☏ *Mon–Sat, 10am–6pm; Sun, 12pm–5pm*

Piccadilly Records
51 Oldham Street
(0161) 839 8008

Piccadilly records has stood proudly on Oldham Street since 1997, in perhaps the only part of the city not dominated by one of the two extremes of towering glass or intimidating-looking local youth hanging around outside with bicycle chains and cheap cider. True to their roots are the staff, who keep it friendly and charming while you rummage around for elaborate looking DJ equipment, clothing or one of their range of gig tickets. As you'd expect, their CD and vinyl stock varies widely and you'd be doing well not to spend the better part of a day browsing the racks.

☏ *Mon & Sat, 10am–6pm; Tue–Fri,*
11am–6pm; Sun, 12pm–5pm

HMV
90–100 Market Street
(0161) 834 8550

Hum Music Vocally. That's what we've been led to believe the initials 'HMV' stand for, and we like to obey this instruction to the letter when stood plugged in to the listening posts.

☏ *Mon, Wed, & Fri–Sat, 9am–6pm; Tue, 9.30am–*
6pm; Thu, 9am–7pm; Sun, 11am–5pm

Virgin Megastore
52–56 Market Street
(0161) 833 1111

Don't feel guilty shopping in big shops. Spend, spend, spend. Buy yourself friends.

☏ *Mon–Sat, 9am–6pm, Sun, 11am–5pm*

Unique Brands at Triangle Shopping Centre — triangle Shopping Centre

Shop

FOOD

The Cheese Hamlet
706 Wilmslow Road, Didsbury
(0161) 434 4781

Cheese connoisseurs and mice rejoice. The Cheese Hamlet, located in the sleepy suburbs of Didsbury, laughingly mocks the anorexic cheese shelf of your local Tesco and Sainsbury's. Expect an interior stocked to the rafters with continental cheeses, Stinky Bishops and far too many options for cheese on toast. We'd like to remind our student readers that cheese on toast can be very satisfying as a breakfast meal, a lunch time snack, a dinner treat or a great post-club feast.

Mon–Wed, 8.30am–5.30pm; Thu–Fri, 8.30am–6.30pm; Sat, 8am–5pm

Eighth Day
111 Oxford Road
(0161) 273 4878

This veggie/vegan shop and caff stocks a chunky selection of foods for those who think baby calves (the animals, not the legs of babies you freaks) are cute, rather than massive burgers with legs on. They do a range of supplements and macrobiotic products to keep your gut's bacterial flora blooming, as well as organic wines and eco-friendly household scrubby stuff. You don't want to dirty your freshly mopped lino with carbon footprints, do you now? We suggest you try their cruelty-free beauty products 'n' all – showing your face without them is cruel to everyone with eyes.

Mon–Tue & Fri–Sat, 9.30am–5.30pm; Wed–Thu, 9.30pm–7pm

Shop

MARKETS

The Arndale Market
Market Hall, Market Street
(0161) 832 3552

It's new. It's bigger. It still smells of fish. The recent extension to the Arndale Centre means that the permanent fixture of the Arndale market becomes um, more permanent and er, bigger. Sorry, we lost our thesaurus when we moved offices. Anyway, the market still packs in the same dubiously cheap clothing and accessories. The overwhelming smell of Grimsby means that you'll probably find a fresh fish shop in the bowels of the market somewhere. Oh well, never mind – we like the smell of the seaside.
◉ *Mon–Sat, 8am–6pm; Sun, 11am–5pm*

Farmers' Market
Piccadilly Gardens
(0161) 234 7356

As we stare out over the sprawling metropolis of Manchester, we can often see green things in the distance. Apparently, these are called 'fields'. It's rumoured that you can 'grow' things in these 'fields'. We thought things grew in the back of Tesco. The farmers' market turns up once every two weeks to mock our city sensibilities and sell us some genuine food. Cheeses, fresh meat, flowers, voluptuous farmers' daughters and magic beans are all on sale, which gives us a chance to try to accustom our digestive tract to something that isn't Smarties cookies.
◉ *2nd & 4th Fri & Sat of the month, 10am–6pm*

French Market
Piccadilly Gardens
(0161) 234 7356

It's desperately tempting to pepper this review with hurtful stereotypes and crass generalisations about our gallic cousins. But no. We at Itchy are bigger than that. Besides, this market is a better advertisement for France than Eric Cantona and Jean Reno ever were. Small but crammed, it's a little taste of the tastiest bits of France, without the painfully annoying but obligatory trial of buying your alcoholic uncle duty free on the way back. Rumours that this market has increased strikes and picket lines by seven percent are unconfirmed. Bollocks, nearly made it. Maybe next year.
◉ *1st Sat of the month, 10am–6pm*

Shop

OTHER

Affleck's Palace
52 Church Street
(0161) 834 1039

When we were wee, we used to sup Tennents Super in the park. It rains too much in Manc for that, so kids have christened Affleck's Palace their home; a multi-floored paradise for those who consider themselves emo, scene, goth, skater or alternative in any way. Small indie stores, a barber's and a café mean that young 'uns need never see the light of day, while piercing and tattoo parlours and fetishwear specialists sort out evening activities for the grown-ups. Now, excuse us, we're off to relive our childhood and drink White Lightning on a set of swings.

Mon–Fri, 10.30am–6pm; Sat, 10am–6pm

Johnny Roadhouse
123 Oxford Road
(0161) 273 1111

If the ménage of hanging instruments sellotaped to the shop exterior didn't give it away, Johnny Roadhouse is the musicians' music shop of music. Whether you play the trombone, clarinet or those weird wooden things on ropes that Crocodile Dundee uses to make a telephone call to his mates, JR (hehe) stocks everything you could need to keep the neighbours up at night. It also has a great choice of secondhand instruments so there's never been a better time to pick up a saxophone and pretend you're in the *Blues Brothers*. Unfortunately, sets of sunglasses don't come as standard.

Mon–Sat, 9.30am–5.30pm

Unique Brands at Triangle Shopping Centre — triangle Shopping Centre

www.itchymanchester.co.uk

Shop

Thunder Egg
First floor, Affleck's Palace
(0161) 835 1019

Yeah, we already mentioned Affleck's, but this place deserves a special hello for its aceness at prezzies. While they don't offer a 'crap gift clearing service', Thunder Egg do stock tons of creative, original trinkets. If you've eaten the girlfriend's dog or forgotten to feed your boyfriend's homework, then nab a thoughtful, unique gift that's 34% better than a Tom Hanks DVD. They also do a small range of clothing if you happen to have crapped your pants worrying about what she'll do when she can't find pooch.

Mon–Fri, 10.30am–6pm; Sat, 10am–6pm

Gash
www.gash.co.uk

When Itchy's mate Dave discovered this über-classy online erotic emporium, stocking lingerie, cosmetics, books, lotions, and lady-pleasing toys including the 'Tongue Joy', he declared, 'That's just like the rhyming kitchen product; Gash – loves the jobs you hate'. This revealed both his dire bedroom prowess and an acute lack of grease-busting knowledge – that's Mr Muscle, not Flash, twazzock. When he's finished with the sink, we've got his girlie some personalised pants to help him patch things up, with a photo of his mug and the words 'Dave, come on down'. Our own deluxe satin pair look stunning, but maybe having them embroidered with 'Itchy' wasn't such a good idea.

Travelling Man
4–4a Dale Street
(0161) 237 1877

You'll like Travelling Man if: you enjoy comic books. You enjoy manga girls. You wish you were Bat/Super/Spiderman. You wish you were a manga girl. You wish you were dating a manga girl (in an obscenely short skirt). You like collecting action figures. You like keeping action figures in their boxes, away from prying hands who would remove them from their boxes, thereby exponentially decreasing their value on eBay. Not that you'll ever let your babies go.

Mon–Sat, 9.30am–6pm;
Sun, 10.30am–4pm

Unique Brands at Triangle Shopping Centre

IF YOU THINK VEGGIES ARE CRANKY, YOU'LL LOVE THIS. FREEGANS SAY OUR ECONOMIC SYSTEM HURTS THE ENVIRONMENT, TREATS ANIMALS CRUELLY AND WORKERS UNFAIRLY, AND WASTES RESOURCES, SO YOU SHOULDN'T PAY FOR FOOD. IDIOTS. HERE'S HOW WE'D BE FREEGANS…

1. Have a Pret dinner – The bods who run Pret a Manger obviously don't know much about the principles of Freeganism, given how much they throw away each day. Turn up at closing, rummage through their bin bags, and hey presto – free dinner.

2. Kill an animal – Apparently it's legal for you to kill squirrels on your own property. With this in mind, set up a bird table, cover it in superglue and get the pot boiling while you wait for it to become a squirrel lolly. Sure, you might snare the odd bird, but extra protein's always welcome, and the RSPB'll never catch you.

3. Forage – Those in the country could nick apples from trees and scour woodland floors for wild mushrooms. Alternatively, those of us whose parents aren't blood-related to each other could pull half-eaten trays of late-night chips from bins.

4. Mug a milkman – Those bastards don't need all that milk. But you do. Being a freegan isn't conducive to a calcium-rich diet, after all. Wait until your local milky's delivering to a dark area, then knock him out and chug as many bottles as you can before making your getaway.

5. Sniper rifle the zoo – Get up high, and train your gun on the elephant cage. It's not going to be easy to take one of those suckers down with one shot, but if it pays off, you'll be eating like a monarch for weeks. Plus you could sell the tusks on to practitioners of Chinese medicine for extra cash.

Freegan fun

Illustration by Thomas Denbigh

www.freegan.info

one Bus Saver

Buy System One Bus Savers where you see this PayPoint sign

Any Bus | Any Train | Any Tram

PP PayPoint

Get out and about with Bus Saver

The only way to get around Greater Manchester on any bus!*

systemonetravelcards.co.uk

*New customers must get a System One membership photocard from a GMPTE Travelshop. All GMPTE Travelshops are PayPoint agents. Bus Savers are accepted by all major local bus companies. Visit systemonetravelcards.co.uk for info or pop into any GMPTE Travelshop.

Out & about

Out & about

CINEMAS

AMC
253 Deansgate
(08707) 555 657

Although you need a map to negotiate the labyrinthine entrance, AMC is a fine film complex if you can manage not to make any David Bowie codpiece jokes. Those who survive the three-day passage to the actual cinema are treated to a plethora of arcade games, friendly staff and an oddly-shaped lobby. It's got all you'd expect from a modern-day, film-showing place (screens and seats and everyfink) and you'll find that the those über-massive packets of popcorn are a little easier on the purse strings. It's fine – we can get obese together.

Mon–Sun, 12pm–1am

The Odeon at The Filmworks
6–8 Dantzic Street
(08712) 244 077

Big things are fun. It's scientifically proven that the bigger something is, the more fun it's going to be. Some examples: tanks, bouncy castles, Peter Kay. The people behind The Filmworks also believe in this ideology. A four hour Peter Jackson epic of a cinema, it has more screens than we can count (seriously – we failed GCSE maths). If there's a film on, you can almost certainly catch it here, so it's perfect for giving in to your partner and taking them to that scintillating Jennifer Aniston rom-com they've been on about seeing. Sadly, Filmworks don't provide ice cream scoops so you can gouge out your eyes during the process.

Mon–Sun, 12pm–1am

The Cornerhouse
70 Oxford Street
(0161) 228 7621

Cornerhouse. A lovely place. You'll leave with a smile upon your face – but if standard fare's what you wish to see, perhaps this ain't your cup of tea. Skip the blockbuster with Tom Hanks; go see films about Spanish banks. Adam Sandler? Why buy tickets? Not when there's documentaries on rickets. Obscure, foreign or animé, animals going all the way. Arty stuff that verges on porn (gents, hide your crotch with your popcorn). Flicks you see to gain respect from those with larger intellect. Black and white or red and violent. Shh! This one's completely silent. And since we're saying 'shh' to you, Itchy will now shut up too.

Mon–Sun, 12pm–8pm

Out & about

COMEDY CLUBS

Frog and Bucket
102 Oldham Street
(0161) 228 6335

Manchester's premium comedy club. Granted, the interior may look like more of a warty toad than a Prince Charming, but this, my friends, is where original comedy is born. Like a maternity ward for popping out jesting stars, but without the fun of rat-wee hospital vending machine-coffee. Its Monday night amateur comedy, 'Beat the Frog', sees Manchester newbies take to the stage in an attempt to make us laugh. You'd never catch Itchy doing that. We have enough of a hard time trying to crowbar jokes into these reviews.

Doors, 7.30pm; Show, 8.30pm–1am

One Night Stand
Bar XS, 343 Wilmslow Road (0161) 257 2403
Opus, The Printworks (0161) 834 2414
Zumeba, 14 Oxford Road (0161) 236 8438

To ensure the Great Drambuie Massacre of 2003 isn't repeated (a disgruntled bar employee, sick of hearing the remix of *Ninety-Nine Red Balloons* covered himself and the entire clientele in 16 bottles of whisky and torched the lot), it's now government policy that bars have at least one night off from loud dance music. Hence, many of Manchester's bars now opt to include a comedy night in their repertoire, and they're usually pretty decent.

Bar XS, Tue; Opus, Fri–Sat; Zumeba, Fri

Jongleurs
40 Chorlton Street
(0870) 787 0707

Even top-flight lawyers and their underpaid secretaries need a giggle occasionally, and Jongleurs is apparently their venue of choice. Washing away a hard day's work of making people bankrupt and answering phones, this club is a favourite of suits and skirts as they try and inject some comedy into their humourless existence, and forget about their erectile dysfunction or the pair of heels they wanged on an already streched-to-maximum credit card this lunchtime. It's not bad though and the drinks are nice enough, but you can't help but feel everyone is smiling merely because it's expected of them. Like at a Labour Party conference.

Sat, 7.30pm 'til late

Get there with system one travelcards.co.uk

www.itchymanchester.co.uk

Out & about

MUSEUMS

Imperial War Museum
Trafford Park
(0161) 836 4000

Edwin Starr posed the eternal question of 'War. What is it good for?'. We smugly point him towards the Imperial War Museum. A fascinating and humbling experience, this is as close as you'll get to battlefields without joining the TA. Or throwing rocks at scallies. An extensive look at the major clashes of the 20th century, it's truly an eye-opening experience and three giant Mars bars better than a stuffy history lecture. Plus you can hone your Winston Churchill impression without looking like a clown.

Mar–Oct, Mon–Sun, 10am–6pm;
Nov–Feb, Mon–Sun, 10am–5pm

Manchester Museum of Science and Industry
Liverpool Road, Castlefield
(0161) 832 2244

Based in the visually stunning Liverpool Road Station, the Museum of Science and Industry is the best school field trip you never had (damn you, box factory). It's an interactive experience more than a museum, 15 galleries packed with state-of-the-art, electronic wizardry inform and entertain on a selection of topics that you mistakenly used to think were dull. Itchy's attempts to construct a space rocket based on the information we got there were sadly fruitless, though that could be due to our incredibly short attention sp... oooh, there's a squirrel in the garden.

Mon–Sat, 10am–5pm

Manchester Museum
University of Manchester, Oxford Road
(0161) 275 2634

If you can sneak down Oxford Road without being spotted by students (a paper bag over your head should do the trick), then you'll find yourself in the Manchester Museum. Samurai swords, mummies and a dinosaur skeleton await those who decide that the educational supplement in the *Daily Mirror* just isn't enough to satisfy their grey muscle. Best of all, it's as free as a computer geek on a Saturday night, so your wallet need not scold you afterwards. Take off the paper bag before you start perusing though. You might knock over a Ming vase or something.

Tue–Sat, 10am–5pm;
Sun–Mon, 11am–4pm

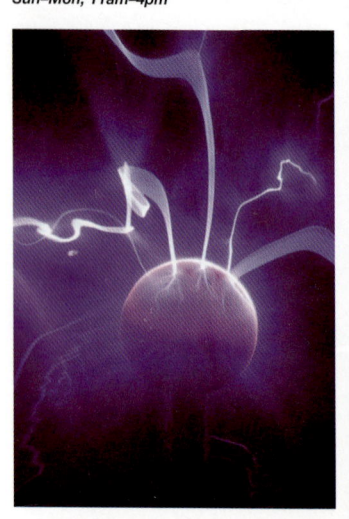

Out & about

GALLERIES

The Cornerhouse
70 Oxford Street
(0161) 228 7621

Don't worry, we won't try and get poetic again. But it is worth knowing that the Cornerhouse provides a small yet fascinating art gallery on the heights of the second floor. Not content with being a bar, restaurant, cinema and detective agency, the venue hosts regular exhibitions. Previous installations have included adorning the restaurant walls with Manga versions of Buddhist gods, so expect the unexpected. Expect the unexpected? Where did we steal that from?

Tue–Sat, 11am–6pm; Thu, 11am–8pm; Sun, 2pm–6pm

The Whitworth
Oxford Road
(0161) 275 7450

It's right in the heart of the student campus, so the major obstacle to making it here is managing to resist the temptation of joining all the undergrads in the nearby pub. A cosy art gallery, usually 'blessed' with a collection of small schoolchildren carrying stinky egg mayo sandwiches in Pokémon lunchboxes, this is a great addition to the art canon of Manchester. Showcasing some of the more unusual exhibitions available to the average Manc on the street, it's undergone a recent regeneration so looks very swish. More swish than the sticky-carpeted, fag-burned dive across the road at any rate.

Mon–Sat, 10am–5pm; Sun, 2pm–5pm

Manchester Art Gallery
Mosley Street
(0161) 235 8888

Paris Hilton could learn a helluva lot from the Manchester Art Gallery. Admittedly, she could learn a lot from primary school too, but we don't have that kind of time. Proving that you don't need to be wearing a scarf and chewing on a pair of spectacles to look intelligent (not that eating eyewear is really too clever), this spot provides an extensive collection of art throughout the ages, with decent guidebooks to help you appreciate the pieces from different perspectives, and it should give you some great ideas for pretty pictures to hang in your bedroom. Don't steal them, though. It's frowned upon.

Tue–Sun, 10am–5pm

www.itchymanchester.co.uk

Out & about

THEATRES

Contact Theatre
Devas Street
(0161) 274 0600

If you flinch at someone saying the word 'vagina' then the Contact probably isn't for you. If you like experimental, often ground-breaking drama and don't grimace at the mention of genitals, then it should be your home from home. Topical, edgy and frequently chuckle-inducing, they regularly host work by new talent, so expect to see the Alan Bennetts of the future here. If you're planning on playing 'spot the newbie screenwriter', they're probably sitting on the front row, nervously eating their cuticles.

Box office, Mon–Sat, 11am–7pm; Doors from 7.30pm

The Lowry
Salford Quays
(08707) 875 780

Take the short ride up to the Quays and conquer your fear of trams. Yes, we're aware 'common' people use them and that they usually toot their horn menacingly at you if you're on the track (usually – sometimes they go right ahead and run you over), but spare us your prejudices and discover the Lowry stage, plonked in the leviathan of the Salford Centre. A modern theatre with the most comfortable seats in the country (we're sure we saw a guarantee there once) and enough plays and acts to distract you from the thought of the dreaded tram ride home. Oh the horror.

Box office, Mon–Sat, 10am–8pm; Sun, 10am–6pm

Let's get physical

Keeping fit: it can be fun. Don't believe us? Then pop over to the **Aquatics Centre** (2 Booth Street East, 0161 275 9450) and sign up for their Body Combat workout. It involves a lot of shouting, punching the air and generally getting yourself knackered in an attempt to relieve stress. Lucy Liu does it, so it must be cool. Plus she's a Charlie's Angel so we wouldn't want to say otherwise lest we get beaten. We enjoy Bollywood dancing. It looks cool. We wish we could dance cool. Thankfully, the **Armitage Centre** (Firs Athletic Ground Moseley Road, 0161 224 0404) have answered our prayers and have set up a Bollywood dance class. Now you too can dance like your favourite Bollywood actors without actually having to burst into song every ten minutes. Woo.

Out & about

The Palace Theatre and The Opera House
Oxford Street (Palace), Quay Street (Opera)
(08704) 013 000

The two premium venues for fans of ballet and iambic pentameter. The Palace is the more mainstream of the two, hosting everything from West End musicals to shows for screaming five year olds. The Opera House is a bit more upmarket and you'll probably catch the latest washed out comic struggling to pay the rent up here. If you fancy a night of sophistication away from the Xbox and drawl of London accents in *Eastenders* then you should head up to these venues pronto. That is, unless you tragically pick a play featuring Dean Gaffney. Playing an Xbox.
Doors, 7.30pm

Royal Exchange Theatre
St Ann's Square
(0161) 833 9833

A landmark of the Deansgate area, The Royal Exchange has been around since the late 60s. Lending its boards to the more original and creative of plays, this is a fine venue for a night of drama, comedy and overpriced bags of Maltesers. It's renowned for nurturing the saplings of fresh talent and regularly hosts writing competitions and workshops, so if you fancy a career change away from licking and sticking envelopes, this could be for you. Although we hear that envelope sticking has great opportunities for career advancement, and you can earn a packet.
Box office, Mon–Fri, 9.30am–7.30am; Sat, 9.30am–8pm

Get there with system one travelcards.co.uk

www.itchymanchester.co.uk

Out & about

LIVE MUSIC

The Academy 1/2/3
Students' Union, Oxford Road
(0161) 275 2930

Academy 1 is the biggest of this trio of venues, located deep in the heart of Studentonia, while visitors to Academy 2 and 3 are likely find the drummer's sweat landing in their plastic cup of beer. Choose from relatively big names or risk it with an unsigned set; you might be able to say that your eardrums were burst by feedback from the next big thing back when they were wee, or maybe just that you were deafened by sonic piss. You could always stand outside the venues and watch the dodgy ticket touts get into scraps with each other, too. That's always entertaining.

Doors, 7.30pm

Bridgewater Hall
Lower Moseley Street
(0161) 907 9000

The civilised side of Manc's music scene. Forget long-haired ruffians and scarf-wearing posers, you're more likely to spot tuxes and gowns in here. If you prefer Beethoven to the Beta Band or Schubert to Snow Patrol, the Bridgewater will verily be a bridge over noisy, insane, thrashily-troubled waters for you. That is, until Classic FM decide to stage a coup, take over the country's airwaves entirely and incarcerate Chris Moyles for crimes against humanity. For folk with refined tastes, this venue should really be better known. Sadly, until Moyles is taken into custody, that may well be just a (pan) pipe dream.

Doors, 7pm

The Green Room
54–56 Whitworth Street West
(0161) 615 0500

Not actually that green, this is an intimate little venue, useful for peering at the music acts of the North West at close range. You could get a really decent aim if they were bad enough to warrant quietly being sniped. Serving up dip-in platters to share of Manchester's hottest talent, the Green Room showcases soulful, wavy-haired ladies caressing acoustic guitars, soulful, mop-haired men murdering acoustic guitars, and many a twenty-Marlboro-a-day voice to growl its way – soulfully – under your skin. Get there early if you want to have a chance of seeing anything but the back of someone's head, however haired.

Doors, 7pm

Out & about

MEN Arena
Victoria Station
(0161) 950 5000

Conveniently located next to Manchester's Victoria station (we suppose when you've just seen Westlife you'll want to scarper as quickly as possible, preferably towards the nearest stiff drink), it's an evening's work for some of the world's biggest stars of music. Although this doesn't necessarily mean best, and while sharing a stadium with the entire population of the British junior school education system is bad enough, it's the screaming parents behind them which really take the custard cream. Ultimately leading us to ask the question: why would any parent ever subject their child to UB40? Red, red whine...

Doors, 7pm

TRAVEL

System One Travelcards
www.systemonetravelcards.co.uk

Having a System One Bus Saver in your wallet is more likely to save your life than a donor card. Ok, so it can't provide you with a pair of shiny new kidneys, but it can get your long-suffering liver back to base on any Greater Manchester bus until 4am, then trundle you to work the next day so all you have to worry about is trying not to breathe your noxious fumes on people. New customers need to take along a passport-sized mugshot (of your face, not your coffee, smart arse) to a GMPTE Travelshop to get a membership card, and after that you can top it up at over 600 PayPoint retailers.

WHAT IS X?   PROMOTION

Throughout 2007, it's the letter that marks the craziest action team, the hottest spots and the most intense evenings of full-on fun.

LuxardoXTeam are on a mystery mission, bar-hopping through the country's most sizzling night zones with games, giveaways, prizes and shots on their X Marks The Spot tour, leaving a trail of unbelievably diamond-hard rocking parties in their wake and teaching the crowd their delicious secrets.

X may be a sambuca-soaked kiss; it might be a target you have to hit to win; it could mark a map with treasure, or be the magic ingredient in a silky, sexy Luxardo Shotail.

The only way to find out is to turn up, and the only way to do that is to check www.LuxardoXTeam.co.uk, where you'll find a full activity calendar, venue listings, galleries, recipes, and competitions with deluxe prizes to be claimed. The rest is yet to be revealed...

LUXARDO
1 8 2 1
SAMBUCA
THE MARK OF SUPERIORITY

www.itchymanchester.co.uk

Out & about

SPORT

Manchester Aquatics Centre
2 Booth Street East
(0161) 275 9450

Those with a passion for inhaling chlorine will love the Aquatics Centre. A mammoth swimming pool, this venue regularly holds water-related sporting activities like swimming or whizzing down the slides. If you don't enjoy organised competitions, you can always just go for a free swim amongst the weeing kids and wrinkly oldies. Make sure you pack water wings for the deep end though. No one wants to see a tubby version of David Hasselhoff jogging towards them in slow motion.
Mon–Fri, 6.30am–10pm; Sat, 7am–6pm; Sun, 7am–10pm

Manchester United Ice Rink
Old Trafford, Sir Matt Busby Way
(0161) 868 8000

Ensuring that we each break at least one bone in our wonder years, giving our mates the chance to draw knobs in felt tip on a cast, the Manchester United Ice rink is a great place to fall over. Here you can slide around to your heart's content until you either get pneumonia or learn to skate like a penguin. Once you're able to skid around without grabbing onto the side for dear life, you're allowed to laugh at people who can't. Not before though. Them's just not Queensberry rules.
Seasonal

The Armitage Centre
Moseley Road, Fallowfield
(0161) 224 0404

Fallowfield. With shedloads of pubs and enough kebab shops to give Jamie Oliver a stroke, one wouldn't be far wrong in suggesting that there's many an XL pair of jeans in these parts. Against this tide of greasy behaviour, the Armitage Centre stands tall, ensuring that at least some of us get to slip into a medium with just a hint of muffin top. A gym, astroturf football pitches, badminton courts, rugby fields and aerobics classes ensure that there's more than enough material here for Johnny Vegas to finally put together that viscose tank top he's always yearned for.
*Mon–Fri, 9.15am–11pm;
Sat–Sun, 10am–8pm*

Manchester United/City
Sir Matt Busby Way, (0161) 868 8000
City of Manchester Stadium, (0870) 062 1894

The mildly pathetic rivalry between the fans of blue and red has been sweating it out for as long as we can remember. Here at Itchy, we want to try and reunite these two tribes by reminding both sets of fans of their similarities, rather than their differences. They both have fantastic grounds. They both support football clubs. They both enjoy beer. They both hate Cristianio Ronaldo. Just like us. Now lets have a hug, join hands and sing rousing folk songs. Or offensive football chants about the French. Whatever.

Get there with system one travelcards.co.uk

Out & about

PAINTBALL AND KARTING

Daytona Indoor Karting
Wharfside Way, Trafford Park
(08456) 445 505

Cars go around in a circle. Fast. Repeat. You don't have to be a rocket scientist to work out how go-karting works. But once you've got that helmet on, worried about the lack of seatbelt and revved the beast of a 50cc engine under your foot, you'll be lost in a world of undertaking, road rage and spinning 360 degrees when you take a corner too fast, your arse within scraping distance of the tarmac. Just remember kids, never try it in a Volvo. Not for safety reasons you understand, but just because you won't look cool.

Mon–Sun, 10am–10pm

Delta Force Paintball
Zulu Wood, Pewit Covert, Brereton Green, Cheshire
(0844) 477 5050

Why can't paintball venues have friendly names? Is a pink flowers and fluffy bunnies paintball business too much to ask? We're sick of typing out these Lynx Java-scented, Tom Clancy-inspired, testosterone-fuelled titles. Regardless, if you enjoy pretending to be Jack Bauer or, um, Ross Kemp, then welcome to the Thunderdome. Strap on a mask, load up your paint-discharging death stick, and run manically around a forest for a day. This is your one opportunity to shout things like 'fire in the hole', 'tango down' or 'damn it, it's encrypted' without looking like an absolute tool, so make the most of it. Hell, do it for PJ.

Mon–Sat, 9.15am–4.30pm

Out & about

Laser Quest
2nd Floor, The Orient, The Trafford Centre
(0161) 755 0600

Frolicking with children hasn't been so much dubious fun since *Heal The World*. Grab yourself a *Ghostbusters* proton pack, make sure your mates know the hand signal for 'flank the chubby kid on the left' and prepare to engage in an exciting game of no physical contact, no crouching, no running, no heavy petting and no hand-to-hand combat. All to a booming selection of high octane trance tracks. Yes, it's childish. Yes, it's probably something you should never tell anyone about. But hot damn if it isn't mildly entertaining to ruin a small child's birthday party by constantly sniping him from the balcony.

Mon–Sun, 10am–11pm

Megabowl
Wilmslow Road, Didsbury
(08715) 501 010

The shudder-inducing notion of rented shoes aside, bowling isn't just a game for single parents and bored children. It's also a game for bored students and lacklustre dates too. Some of Itchy's most intense existential panics have been induced by being presented with limp, over-priced, insipid chicken in a basket at bowling lanes. In defence, there are few finer feelings than rolling a spherical mass down an alley and getting a strike. Indeed, the chances of this happening are greatly increased if you roll two balls down the alley at the same time. Three's just greedy.

Mon–Thu & Sun, 12pm–12am;
Fri, 12pm–1am; Sat, 10am–1am

Out & about

FURTHER AFIELD

Heaton Hall
Heaton Park, Middleton Road, Prestwich
(0161) 773 1231

Comprising 25% of Manchester's green space (the other 75% is in a warehouse in Hulme), Heaton Hall and Park scares us. Maybe it's the spooky mansion. Maybe we're afraid of their spectacular firework displays. Or maybe we're just scared of grass. Whatever the case, we're willing to face our fears and enjoy this splendid day out. Rolling scenery. Old codgers walking. The smell of oxygen. It's like being in a Jane Austen novel without all the uncomfortable corsets and inappropriate advances of people in crotch-hugging jodphurs.

Mon–Sun, 11am–5.30pm

Jodrell Bank Science Centre and Arboretum
Macclesfield, Cheshire
(01477) 571 321

Telescopes: no longer used only for spying on your neighbours. Jodrell Bank is home to Manchester University's telescope. They use it for looking at planets, stars and probably not for watching next-door's Sky TV. Now, you too can pretend to be a physicist. Don a lab coat, take the guided tour and tut obnoxiously when someone mentions that Pluto is no longer a planet. There's also a collection of Malus and Sorbus in the grounds. We don't really know what they are though, although they sound quite dirty and something you should probably wear wellies for.

Mon–Sun, 10.30am–5.30pm

Half an hour of fun

Loads of Northern Quarter bars have a fine selection of 'literature' for you to peruse if you've got time to kill. **Odd Bar** (30–32 Thomas Street, 0161 833 007) and **Pop Boutique** (34–36 Oldham Street, 0161 236 5797) make killer coffee, plus you'll never run out of magazines to read. Unless you read scarily fast. Or just look at the pictures. You freak. **Piccadilly Gardens** offers some great places to sit and watch the world/pigeons go by. There are normally people giving out free papers so grab one and read how morality is declining. There's a popular theory going round that the television in **Exchange Square** was erected for just such an occasion as this. Take a pew and watch the news, *Neighbours* or whatever home improvement show the BBC broadcast at three o'clock in the afternoon.

www.itchymanchester.co.uk

Out & about

Liverpool
www.itchyliverpool.co.uk

Less than an hour away travelling on the marvellous and not-at-all-late British rail system, and possibly quicker if you send yourself via Parcelforce, Liverpool is the second best city around these parts. Home to the Beatles, a sheep shaped like a banana and Liverpool FC, it's an ideal break if you need an escape from the urban heat of Manchester. They turned the urban heat down in Scouseland since they discovered how flammable shell suits are. Clearly, we can't list all the best venues the city has here, but most conveniently, the Itchy Guide to Liverpool should have all that covered. You know, just in case you fancy picking one up. And paying for it. Don't get too much into the Liverpool spirit, now.

The Trafford Centre
(0161) 749 1717

Probably responsible for more than a couple of repossession notices, this monster shopping centre can eat up days without much effort. Aside from gadzillions of shops, there's a restaurant area shaped like a ship, fountains in which you can throw your pennies and make a wish (most likely that you didn't throw them in the first place – you'll need them when the Visa bill arrives), and a multi-screen cinema which provides a great opportunity to rest your knackered legs and enjoy some escapism at the end of your trip. Don't bother with the last screenings though if you'd rather avoid a back row full of chavs smoking weed.

☻ *Mon–Fri, 10am–10pm; Sat, 10am–8pm; Sun, 12pm–6pm*

Get there with system one travelcards.co.uk

Stag & hen

Illustration by Thomas Denbigh

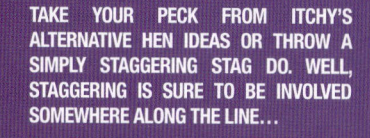

TAKE YOUR PECK FROM ITCHY'S ALTERNATIVE HEN IDEAS OR THROW A SIMPLY STAGGERING STAG DO. WELL, STAGGERING IS SURE TO BE INVOLVED SOMEWHERE ALONG THE LINE…

Unless the bride/groom's into the type of swinging that doesn't happen in park play areas (if it does – hell, you need to move to a better estate), by saying 'I do' your friend is promising not to indulge in bratwurst boxing with anyone but their chosen partner. For £52 per person, you can make sure they pack in the porking prior to the big day at a sausage-making course (www.osneylodgefarm.co.uk), and fry up the results the morning after to calm your hangovers.

As they're already selflessly donating themselves to someone else for life, chuck some extra charity in the mix; if you can raise enough cash for a good cause, experiences like bungee jumping, fire walking and skydiving are absolutely free. Wedding guests could pledge sponsorship as part of their gifts to the couple, and the money saved could go towards an extra few days on the honeymoon. Suitable charities for those getting hitched to munters include the Royal National Institute of the Blind or Battersea Dogs' Home.

PASSION FOR MUSIC, PASSION FOR LIFE

www.galaxyfm.co.uk

Galaxy

GALAXY IS AVAILABLE ON FM, DAB DIGITAL RADIO AND SKY / NTL/ TELEWEST

Laters

Laters

Basket case

Those of you who've forgotten to buy the essential ingredients for that perfect slice of toast need not fear the coming of the witching hour. Manchester has plenty of late night stores to cater for all sorts of cravings. Nip up to the Tesco superstore in Didsbury to find a 24-hour neon-lit paradise. If you don't intend to do your whole weekly shop, the Tesco market in Fallowfield stays open to the early hours. Closer to town, the Spar on Oxford Road (opposite the Beeb) keeps its doors open to any latecomers, if you just can't shake the desire for a bottle of strawberry milk.

Nightly nicotine

If you don't want to have your wallet helpfully cleaned out by one of those extortionately priced cigarette machines humming innocently in the corner of most bars, nip out to one of these. Somerfield in central Piccadilly stays open until 10pm every weekday, so you can stock up on shower gel as well as Marlie lights, and the Aleef store in the Printworks remains open until 2am on Friday and Saturday for post-club addicts. Down in darkest Fallowfield, try the 24-hour Total Petrol Station on Wilmslow Road, but keep your gaspers well out of sight of scroungers, they're precious goods first thing in the morning.

Feed me now

O-live while you're alive and sleep when you're dead - Olive Deli on Whitworth Street is open until 10pm every day for you to marinade yourself in sunblush deliciousness and get pickled on vodka with more kick than Bruce Lee reincarnated as an angry donkey. In the city centre, plump for Leo's fish bar on Oldham Street and show a burger a good time. McTucky's fried chicken on Canal Street is also good for hot birds. Ahem. In Rusholme, opt for Caspians. If you've dared trek to Fallowfield, we'd happily point you towards Mamma Mia's pizza. Then the nearest bus or taxi out of there.

Civilised cuisine

If you don't really fancy wiping tomato ketchup and spilt kebab onto the back of your jeans, you may be wanting the services of a late night restaurant. If your taste buds yearn for spicy nirvana, Curry Mile in Rusholme can happily oblige. Many of the curry houses in this part of town are open 'til 3am, but we'd suggest ignoring the first one you come to and trying Al-Bilal. If you want to throw noodles at each other, pop up to Shang Hi Buffet Restaurant on Whitworth Street. It's open until 11pm to cater for those of you who've forgotten to eat dinner before drinking seven pints.

Laters

Get in the spirit

If the party's suffered a breakdown in the early hours due to alcohol deficiency, then Crateman have the liq-cure (0870 950 1525/www.crateman.co.uk). Their ace alcohol ambulance delivers everything from beer, Bolly and bottles to fresh limes for your Corona, Pringles and smokes between 11pm–6am, Fri–Sat and 11pm–4am, Sun–Thu. Call centre staff are trained to translate the arseholed sound of you trying to French kiss your mobile into a polite request for a crate of Magners, four Red Bulls and a litre of fresh OJ, and will even guarantee a time by which the goodies will arrive at your door.

Clubbing around the clock

If the dreaded 2am bell has tolled and you still want to try and dance like your dad, there are a couple of dancefloors around this thumping city that will oblige you well into the wee hours. Jilly's Rockworld holds a Friday 'All Nighter' event, which pumps out all the old rock 'classics' until 7am. Next door, The Music Box normally keeps people flowing in until 4am or 5am on a weekend, depending on the event. Saturday revellers might want to check out Sankey's, which broadcasts brain-mashing techno and dance tunes until the milkman does the rounds at 5am.

Late licences

There are many reasons as to why someone would want to consume the demon drink after the bell's been rung for last orders and luckily there are plenty of late license establishments to aid you in your goal of splattering the kerb with a coat stomach paint. **Kro Piccadilly** (1 Piccadilly Gardens) is slap bang in the centre of town, and only starts clearing out the drunks at 2am. If you're looking for a less rowdy pint stroll to **Mojo** (19 Back Bridge Street) or **Bluu** (Smithfield Market Buildings) for late drinking, without the impending threat of getting chatted up by a scallie. Away from the tits and teeth of the city centre lies the student hub of Fallowfield, although you may need to flash your student card at the door to gain entry to its drinking nirvanas like **The Cheshire Cat** or **The Orange Grove**.

www.itchymanchester.co.uk

Laters

Fashionistas' friends

If you've accidentally poured a brew down that killer dress or shirt or you've forgotten to wash your underwear for that big night out, never fear. The Arndale Centre keeps its automatic doors open until 8pm on weekdays so you've got plenty of time to nip to Topshop, River Island and the like. If the tumble dryer hasn't got your party ensemble dry by the evening, the shopping paradise of the Trafford Centre burns the candle until 10pm, so you can manage a mad dash around in order to find a replacement. Because no one likes to go clubbing wearing a pair of wet, squelchy socks.

Midnight movies

If you can't stand the idea of watching the latest blockbuster with a bunch of screaming kids, then the Printworks and the AMC keep the reels, um, reeling way past bed time. The last screenings are at around 12am at weekends.

Snake eyes

If you think you can do a better job than Bond himself, then Manchester has a number of late night casinos to blow your pennies in. Mint Casino on Princess Street and Circus Casino on Portland Street stay open 'til 6am, Mon–Sat and 4am on Sun.

Fun @ night

DON'T WASTE THE GIFT OF INSOMNIA BY COUNTING IMAGINARY ANIMALS – GO CREATE SOME SHEAR (ARF) MAYHEM IN THE EARLY AM AND ENTER THE ITCHY TWILIGHT ZONE. WE WOOL IF YOU WOOL

Go jousting – First up, feed up for some insane-sbury's prices. As witching hours approach, 24-hour supermarkets reduce any unsold fresh produce to mere coppers; pick up a feast for a few pauper's pennies and buy them clean out of 10p French sticks, which are spot on for sword fights. Up the ante by jousting using shopping trolleys or bicycles in place of horses, or start a game of ciabatta-and-ball by bowling a roll.

Play street games – Take some chalk to sketch a marathon hopscotch grid down the entire length of the thoroughfare, or an anaconda-sized snakes and ladders board writhing across your town square. Break the trippy silence and deserted stillness of the dead shopping areas with a tag, catch or British bulldog competition, and be as rowdy as you like – there's no-one around to wake.

Play Texaco bingo – Alternatively, drive the cashier at the all-night petrol station honey nut loopy by playing Texaco bingo: the person who manages to make them go back and forth from the window the most times to fetch increasingly obscure, specific and embarrassing items wins. Along with your prize-winning haul of mango chutney-flavoured condoms, Tena Lady towelettes and tin of eucalyptus travel sweets, be sure to pick up a first-edition paper to trump everyone over toast with your apparently psychic knowledge of the day ahead's events-to-be. Whatever you do, remember: you snooze, you lose.

Illustration by Thomas Denbigh

AA driving school

enjoy

Buy 2 AA driving lessons and get 1 FREE*.

Don't miss out! Book your first lesson today.
Call 0800 107 2044.

www.AAdrivingschool.co.uk

AA driving school. Drive your dreams forward

FREE AA DRIVING LESSON

Your FREE AA driving lesson voucher

Book your first lessons today.
Call 0800 107 2044. Buy 2 lessons, then simply hand this voucher to your AA driving instructor at your first lesson to arrange your free lesson.

Your Name	(Instructor use only) AA Driving Instructor Name
Your Pupil Number	AA Driving Instructor Number

(Given on calling 0800 107 2044)

*Offer closes 31st March 2008. Only 1 free hour of tuition will be given per pupil. Offer not available to existing AA driving school pupils and cannot be used in conjunction with any other offer. Offer subject to instructor availability. AA driving instructors are self-employed franchisees and all contracts for the provision of driving tuition are between the pupil and the instructor. Only one voucher redeemable per pupil. Full terms and conditions are available at www.AAdrivingschool.co.uk

Code 342 – Itchy

Sleep

Sleep

SWANKY

Britannia Hotel
35 Portland Street
(0161) 236 9154

Located near the shopping haven of Market Street, this listed building is perfect for shopaholics. It's also real pretty.
£70–£135

The Hilton
303 Deansgate
(0161) 870 1650

Ignore the fact that you're probably paying for one of Ms. Hilton's manicures and relax in this shiny, monstrosity of an establishment. This is a 'premium hotel', and at these prices it really should be.
£116

The Lowry
50 Dearmans Place
(0161) 827 4000

This glamorous hotel has more awards than Stephen Fry's groaning Bafta shelf. Just ignore the cries of agony coming from your purse and pay a visit to the on-site gym, spa and health rooms.
£120–£370

Victoria & Albert Hotel
Water Street
(0161) 832 1188

Although it's quite doubtful that Queen Vic or her hubby ever stayed here, you can comfort yourself with the prospect of having a Playstation in every room. Unfortunately you can't take it with you when you leave.
£135–£225

MID-RANGE

The Castlefield Hotel
Liverpool Road
(0161) 832 7073

This joint's a decent three-star hotel with a pool, sauna and running track to tire you out before bed, don'tcher know.
From £90

The Golden Tulip
Trafford Park
(0161) 873 8899

An entirely non-smoking hotel, the Golden Tulip is a comfortable place, away from the manic hustle and bustle of Manchester central. There's a restaurant and bar in the complex, so you need never leave.
£55–£195

Holiday Inn
Liverpool Street
(0161) 743 0080

Whatever parent you decide to tap up for the cash, you can be sure of a hearty breakfast and a night dreaming about soft, fluffy bunnies or something equally small and cute. Like kittens. Or Ronnie Corbett.
£63–£115

Princess Hotel
101 Portland Street
(0161) 236 5122

A home from home. This hotel is ideal for those not wanting to sacrifice a goat to Satan to afford the room rates. Each room has a large satellite television, data port and nice downy beds for the snoozy traveller.
£77–£118

Sleep

CHEAP

The Chesters Hotel
730 Chester Road
(0161) 236 5122
A great value three star hotel in the heart of Old Trafford. A snazzy little restaurant and affordable room rates make it a real find.
💷 *£55–£90*

Ibis Hotel
96 Portland Street
(0161) 272 5000
Not the swankiest hotel we've ever stayed in but efficiently comfortable and much better than the street benches outside. Pets are allowed so Daisy the dog need not be kept at Aunt Lizzie's for the weekend.
💷 *£55*

Stay Inn
55 Blackfriars Road
(0161) 907 2277
While the temptations of an en-suite bathroom and a hairdryer might not be enough to persuade you to Stay In (hur-hur) your room all day, this is a nice enough hotel for a whistle-stop tour around Manchester.
💷 *£18.33*

Walkabout Hotel
13 Quay Street
(0161) 817 4800
An Australian-themed hotel, though those of you expecting hammocks and kangaroos will be sorely disappointed. Those of you expecting beds and en-suite tea and coffee facilities will be very content.
💷 *£50*

Dolby Hotel
55 Blackfriars Road
(0161) 907 2277
Five-star it ain't, but at these prices, you'd have to be mental to expect it to be. It's clean, it's cheap and it's not far from the train station. And it's got sod all to do with stereo sound, before you ask.
💷 *From £41*

Premier Travel Inn
112–114 Portland Street
(0161) 272 5000
Probably the nicest of the budget hotels on offer in Manchester. High speed internet access, a nice view of the city and a collection of pillows mean you need never go out, but then what's the point of this guide?
💷 *£58*

Travelodge
Blackfriars Road
(0870) 191 1659
Plumped in the Deansgate area of Manchester, this hotel does exactly what it says on the um, sign. Lodging for travellers. It's cheap and cheery, though don't expect to see any celebrities or film stars.
💷 *£50*

The Wilmslow Hotel
356 Wilmslow Road
(0161) 225 3030
Great for when you've got more mates visiting than spare sofas. It's not particularly spectacular but when you really just need to crash after a night on the pop, are you honestly looking for an en-suite Jacuzzi?
💷 *£25–£65*

www.itchymanchester.co.uk

Dos & don'ts

Illustration by Si Clark, www.si-clark.co.uk

EVER NOTICE HOW THE IMPORTANT STUFF IN LIFE ALWAYS SEEMS TO BE THE MOST BORING? TAKE FLAT HUNTING – PRETTY SIGNIFICANT, BUT ABOUT AS THRILLING AS WATCHING THE PAINT DRY ON A PICTURE OF STEVE 'INTERESTING' DAVIS. TO HELP YOU OUT, HERE'S ITCHY'S DOS AND DON'TS OF RENTING...

# of renting

DO read everything. Your tenancy agreement/contract may not have a through-line as gripping as *The Da Vinci Code*'s, but it should be treated as your holy text.

DO ask. Ensure that you consult your landlord before making any changes.

DO get an inventory. No matter how long your tenancy, you want to know what was there when you moved in and (more importantly) if it was looking as crappy then as it does now you're moving out.

DO keep an eye out for any damp, damage and general disrepair when viewing properties.

DON'T be afraid of looking like an asshole for asking too many questions about boring things. Get hold of those valid certificates for gas appliances, whatever you do.

DON'T move into an area blind. Ask around to see what it's like.

DON'T be fooled by a new paint job. In pretty much the opposite of a famous Michael Barrymore TV advertising mantra for chocolate biccies, it might be all white, but that don't mean that it's alwight.

DON'T go getting hammer happy on the walls. Crying when you end up losing your deposit won't help.

Know your rights

IF YOU FIND YOURSELF CAUGHT IN A STICKY SITUATION, MAKE SURE YOU GET YOURSELF STRAIGHT ON TO THE FOLLOWING:

Shelter (it's not just for the homeless, you know) – *www.shelter.org.uk/advice*
Association of Residential Letting Agents – *www.arla.co.uk*
Citizens' Advice Bureau – *www.citizensadvice.org.uk*

Itchy

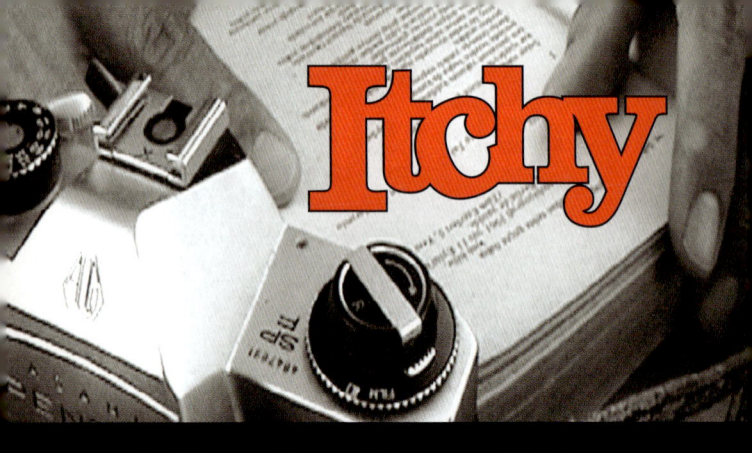

Calling all aspiring scribblers and snappers...

We need cheeky writers and hawk-eyed photographers to contribute their sparkling talents to the Itchy city guides and websites. We want the inside track on the bars, pubs, clubs and restaurants in your city, as well as longer features and dynamic pictures to represent the comedy, art, music, theatre, cinema and sport scenes.

If you're interested in getting involved, please send examples of your writing or photography to: editor@itchymedia.co.uk, clearly stating which city you can work in. All work will be fully credited.

**Bath/Birmingham/Brighton/Bristol/Cambridge/Cardiff/Edinburgh/
Glasgow/Leeds/Liverpool/London/Manchester/
Nottingham/Oxford/Sheffield/York**

www.itchycity.co.uk

Useful info

Useful info

BEAUTY SALONS

Didsbury Beauty Clinic
715a Wilmslow Road, Didsbury
(0161) 445 4147

Do people laugh at you when you walk down the street? You need help, fast.
Tue–Thu, 10am–8pm; Fri, 10am–6pm; Sat, 9am–4pm

The Lowry Health Spa
Lowry Hotel, Dearmans Place, Chapel Wharf, Salford
(0161) 827 4034

All manner of modern beauty tomfoolery, so you can be looking your best for that office night out. You'll still look funny with a facial mask on though. It's unavoidable.
Mon–Fri, 7am–10pm;
Sat–Sun, 8am–8pm

HAIRDRESSERS

Toni and Guy Academy
Queens House, Queen Street
(0161) 832 8282

Toni and Guy newbies learn to cut hair on willing victi... um, volunteers. That said, you'll get a quality snip for half the price.
Mon–Fri, 9am–5.30pm

Olivier Morosini
98 Tib Street
(0161) 832 8989

Best for barnets, bar none. All stylists are senior, giving full consultations and friendly, personal service, so you actually get what you wanted: some hair left, that looks great.
Mon–Wed, 9am–6pm; Thu, 10am–8pm;
Fri, 9.30am–6pm; Sat, 9am–4pm

TANNING

The Sun Room
87 Mauldeth Road
(0161) 224 4330

Not a tabloid newspaper in sight in this nice and simple tanning parlour. Perfect for a bit of pre-summer bronzing.
Mon–Sat, 9am–5pm

Sun City
38 John Dalton Street
(0161) 834 7777

Never has there been a more ironic name for a shop based in Manchester. Sun City allows you to copy David Dickinson without the tedium of selling antiques. You know when you've been Tangoed? Quite.
Mon–Sat, 9am–5pm

GYMS

GL-14
3 Chepstow Street
(0161) 228 6789
Modern gym complete with those odd physio balls that no one knows how to work.
Mon–Thu, 6.30am–10pm;
Sat–Sun, 9am–6pm

Monty's Health and Fitness Club
21–23 Oldham Street
(08005) 424 749
A ladies-only gym, slap-bang in the city centre, with over 20 fitness classes for people scared of rowing machines.
Mon & Wed, 7am–9.30pm; Tue & Thu–Fri, 10am–9.30pm; Sat–Sun, 10am–4pm

Virgin Active
1 Great Northern Warehouse, Deansgate
(0161) 831 0600
Christ, is there any pie old Branson doesn't have his finger in? A massivo gym with weight rooms, an 'energy bar' and internet access. Presumably so you can look at pictures of cake while you run.
Mon–Fri, 6.30am–9pm; Sat–Sun, 9am–5pm

The Y Club
Liverpool Road
(0161) 837 3535
Sauna, gym, steam room, personal trainers, weights, rowing machines, sports hall, swimming pool, fitness classes, indoor running track, kitchen sink.
Mon–Fri, 6am–10pm; Sat, 8am–8pm;
Sun, 8am–7pm

ESTATE AGENTS

M1 City Apartments
68 Whitworth Street West
(0161) 228 1877
www.ls-1.co.uk
If pads really did come padded, the plush apartments this city centre specialist offers would be the snuggliest, fluffiest cashmere comfort blankets ever. The excellent M1 'life agents' cater for those who want to rent or buy right in the heart of Manc's chest. Live somewhere with proper interior design that extends beyond putting a poster over the hole in the wall you where you whacked it with the door handle, and a bowl of mouldy pot pourri on top of the bit of sideboard you accidentally burnt with a joss stick.
Mon–Fri, 9am–6pm; Sat, 10am–4pm

www.itchymanchester.co.uk

Inviting guys back for coffee wouldn't be such hard work if I lived in the city, pondered Bertha.

Living in the city means getting back to your pad after a night out is a breeze, with friends or otherwise! In an über stylish M1 apartment you'll be slap-bang in the centre of all that Manchester has to offer - cool bars, swanky restaurants, trendy shops, funky clubs and celeb spotting opportunities galore. Add to that world class cultural, sporting and music venues and there simply isn't a more vibrant place to live. So what are you waiting for? Come out of the middle of nowhere and into the middle of everything!

Just call one of our life agents on **0161 228 1877**; they're the most clued up 'movers and shakers' on the residential market.

city apartments life agents, not just estate agents

sales & rentals **t 0161 228 1877** M1, 68 whitworth street west, manchester M1 5WW.

Useful info

TAKEAWAY CURRY

Abduls
133–135 Oxford Road, All Saints
(0161) 273 7339

We'd advise against trying to eat a chicken korma out of your lap when you're rip-roaring drunk. Seriously, you should see our pants.

Mon–Sun, 12pm–12am

Spicy Hut Restaurant
35 Wilmslow Road
(0161) 248 6200

Takeaway from a tasty Rusholme curry house. Perfect if you fancy a night in front of the television or luminous fish tank. Plus, they do free delivery within one mile. Perfect if you've lost your shoes.

Mon–Sun, 12pm–12am

TRAVEL ESSENTIALS

GMPTE Information Line
(0161) 228 7811

They'll tell you how far you can get for 50p. Probably not as far as your mate's cousin will let you go for a fiver and a blue WKD, but a much safer way to get back to your bed.

Mon–Fri, 7am–8pm; Sat–Sun, 8am–8pm

System One Travelcards
www.systemonetravelcards.co.uk

1, 7, and 28-day cards available, plus annual passes, all of which let you take any bus, anytime, anywhere. You won't have felt such intense love for plastic since that devastatingly attractive inflatable sheep. Party 'til the wheels fall off without worrying about saving cash for the ride home.

TAKEAWAY PIZZA

Buy The Slice
2 Chapel Street
(0161) 832 5553

Grab a monster 19" pizza, get some mates around and pretend you're in *Friends*. Without the naked guy opposite, we hope.

Mon–Sun, 11.30am–11.30pm

Domino's
224 Wilmslow Road
(0161) 257 3832

Crawling with lazy students who forgot to buy dinner, Domino's does your typical takeaway fare. They also deliver if you can't be bothered to dig out your slippers from under the bed.

Mon–Sun, 12pm–11pm

TRAINS

National Rail Enquiries
(08457) 484 950

Fancy a chat with a crazy person? Catch a train and sit on one of the seats next to a table. Pretty soon, your mad companion won't be the only person frothing at the mouth.

Daily, 24 hours

Virgin Trains
(08457) 222 333

Virgin are onto something here. They make special trains that are designed to tilt round corners, which means they're much faster. Unless of course there's a delay due to signal failure, leaves on the line, passenger action, privatisation, or any of the other reasons the trains in this country are so crap.

www.itchymanchester.co.uk

Useful info

BUSES

National Express
Chorlton Street
(08705) 808 080

Comfy travel for those of you who like motorways, dodgy service stations and bored children kicking the back of your seat.
Enquiry Line, 8am–10pm

Piccadilly Bus Station
Piccadilly Gardens
(0161) 228 7811

The double decker hub of Manchester. The late buses are a godsend to all the drunks of the world, getting legless people home at all hours. Not that we ever get so drunk that we can't walk, obviously. Ahem.
Mon–Sun, 8am–8pm

INTERNET CAFÉS

Easy Internet Café
8 Exchange Square
(0161) 832 9200

344 computers, so you can be pretty sure of being able to send that email to your uncle Toby. Or play online games. Whatever.
Mon–Fri, 8am–10pm; Sat–Sun, 9am–9pm

Mak's Internet Café
65 Blackfriars Road
(0161) 835 1899

Seven stations for all your 'I wonder what's happening on *Big Brother* now' needs. Printing and refreshments also available. Just don't spill Coke on the keyboard.
*Mon–Fri, 10am–9pm;
Sat–Sun, 10am–6pm*

CAR HIRE

Hertz Car Rentals
Manchester Airport, Terminal One
(0870) 850 8784

According to R.E.M., Everybody Hertz sometimes. Which strikes us as being very unfair to non-drivers who never Hertz. Didn't think about that, did you baldie?

TAXIS

Avenue Cars
16a Victoria Avenue
(0161) 740 3030

Manchester Cars
70 Portland Street
(0161) 236 3555

LAUNDRETTES

Granada Dry Cleaners
71–73 Bridge Street
(0161) 834 8947

Ensuring we all go to work, weddings and movie premiers looking snazzy and suave, with same day service for the disorganised.
Mon–Sat, 9am–5pm

The Laundry Room
839 Wilmslow Road
(0161) 445 6264

Our laundry room is full of odd socks and for some reason, plant pots. Anyway, expect none of that here. Suits pressed, shined and looking like you bought them from Primark only yesterday.
Mon–Sat, 9am–5pm

Support

Illustration by Joly Braime

Brook Advisory Centre
Commonwealth House, Lever Street
(0161) 237 3001

Greater Manchester Police
(0161) 856 0905

Manchester City Council
Town Hall, Albert Square
(0161) 234 5000

Manchester Drug Service
The Bridge, 104 Fairfield Street
(0161) 273 4040

Manchester Royal Infirmary
Oxford Road Manchester
(0161) 276 1234

Manchester University Police Liaison Officer
(0161) 275 7042

Manchester Visitors Centre
Lloyd Street, St Peter's Square
(08712) 228 223

NHS Direct
(0845) 46 47

Samaritans
72–74 Oxford Street
(08457) 909 090

Trafford Alcohol Services
Cornhill Clinic, Cornhill Road
(0161) 747 1841

www.itchymanchester.co.uk

Get there with system **one** travelcards.co.uk

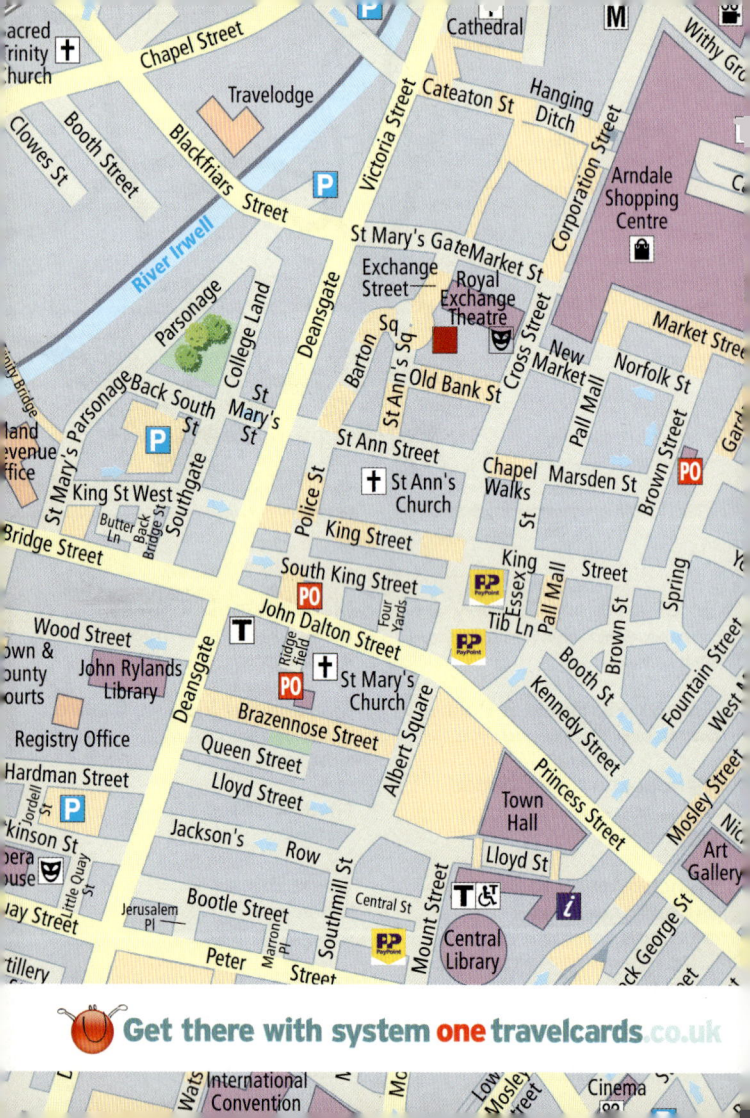

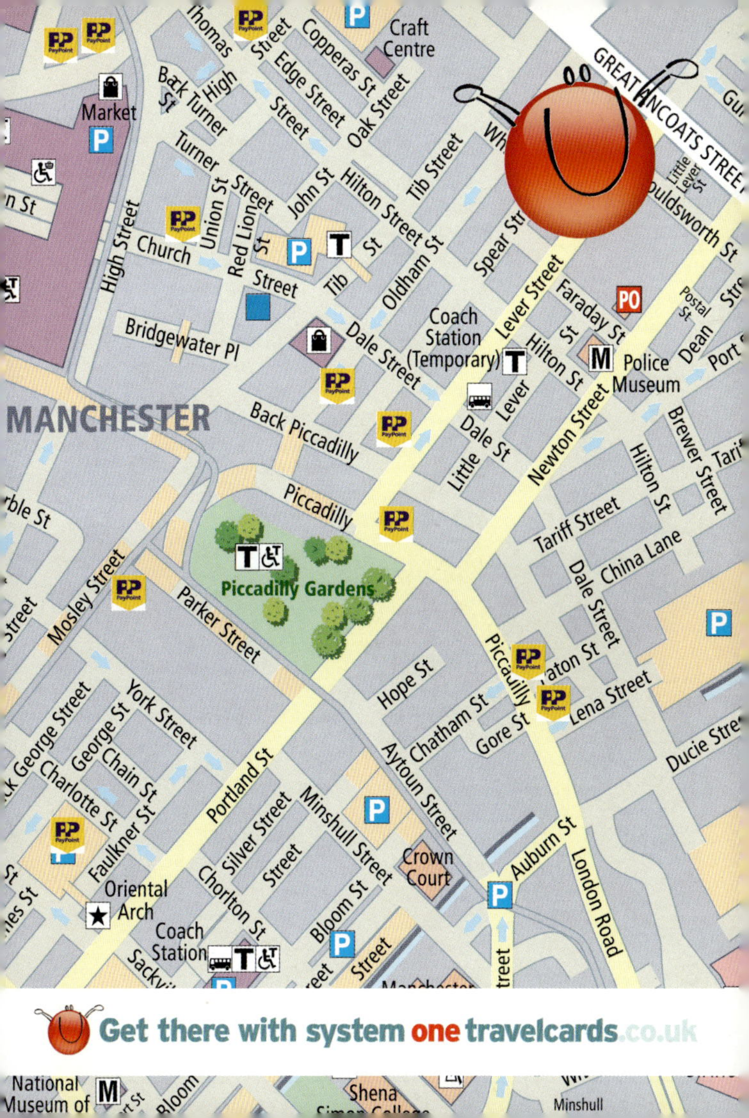
MANCHESTER
Piccadilly Gardens
Craft Centre
Market
Coach Station (Temporary)
Police Museum
Oriental Arch
Coach Station
Crown Court
National Museum of
GREAT ANCOATS STREET
Copperas St
Edge Street
Oak Street
Thomas Street
High Street
Back Turner St
Turner Street
Union St
Red Lion St
John St
Hilton Street
Tib Street
Tib St
Oldham St
Spear St
Lever Street
Faraday St
Hilton St
Goulsworth St
Little Lever St
Postal St
Dean
Port
Church Street
High Street
Bridgewater Pl
Dale Street
Dale St
Little Lever
Back Piccadilly
Piccadilly
Newton Street
Brewer Street
Hilton St
Tariff Street
China Lane
Dale Street
Mosley Street
Parker Street
Hope St
Chatham St
Gore St
Lena Street
Ducie Street
Piccadilly
York Street
George St
Chain St
Charlotte St
Faulkner St
Portland St
Silver Street
Minshull Street
Aytoun Street
Auburn St
London Road
Chorlton St
Bloom St
Sackville
Minshull
Bloom
PO
PayPoint

Index

42nd Street	56
5th Avenue	56

A

The Academy 1/2/3	94
Affleck's Palace	83
Al Bilal	13
AMC	88
Ampersand	56
The Armitage Centre	96
The Arndale Market	82
The Assembly Bar & Grill	41
The Athenaeum	36
Atlas	30
The Attic	56
AXM	66

B

The Bank	36
Bar XS	42
The Bar	32
Barca	30
The Bay Horse	46
BED	57
The Beech Inn	33
Beluga	13
Blackwells	79
Bluu (Bar)	14 & 46
Bluu (Clothing)	74
Borders	78
Bouzouki by Night	14
The Bridge	36
Bridgewater Hall	94
Britannia Hotel	110
Britons Protection	37

C

Café Istanbul	14
Café Muse	10
Café Pop	10
Casa Tapas	15
Cast	74
The Castlefield Hotel	110
The Cavendish	51
Che	34
The Cheese Hamlet	81
The Cheshire Cat	44
The Chesters Hotel	111
Clone Zone	68
Club Alter Ego	67
Club V	57
Common	46
Contact Theatre	92
The Cornerhouse	48, 88 & 91
Croma	15

D

Darbar	15
Daytona Indoor Karting	97
Deansgate	72
Delta Force Paintball	97
Didsbury Village Restaurant	15
Dimitri's Taverna	16
The Dog & Patridge	41
Dolby Hotel	111
Domino's	119
The Drop Inn	52
Dukes 92	31

E

Easy Internet Café	120
Eden Bar	66
Eighth Day	12 & 81
Essential Nightclub	67
Est Est Est	16
Evuna	17

F

Fab Café	34
The Famous Trevor Arms	33
Farmer's Market	82
Felicini	17
Font Bar	48
Fopp	80
Four in Hand	52
French Market	82
French Restaurant	18
Friendship Inn	44
Frog and Bucket	89

G

Gash	84
Gaucho Grill	18
Gemini Café	10
Glass	42
The Golden Tulip	110
Granada Dry Cleaners	120
The Green Room	94
The Greenhouse	18
The Grill on the Alley	19
Grinch	20

H

Hardy's Well	51
Harvey Nichols	73
Heaton Hall	99
Hertz Car Rentals	120
The Hilton	110
HMV	80
Holiday Inn	110
The Horse and Jockey	33

I

Ibis Hotel	111
Imperial War Museum	90

Index

J

Jabez Clegg	57
Jake Shoes	77
Jazz	76
Jilly's Rockworld	58
Jodrell Bank	99
Johnny Roadhouse	83
Jongleurs	89

K

Knott Bar	30
The Koffee Pot	10
Koreana	19
Kro Bar	20
Kro Piccadilly	35
Kro2	48

L

Laser Quest	98
Le Mont	21
The Lead Station	32
Life Café	38
The Living Room	38
Loaf	38
Lotus Bar and Dim Sum	21
The Lowry (Theatre)	92
The Lowry Hotel	110

M

M1 City Apartments	117
M2	58
Mak's Internet Café	120
Malmaison Brasserie	21
Manchester Aquatics Centre	96
Manchester Art Gallery	91
Manchester Cars	120
Manchester Museum	90
Manchester Museum of Science and Industry	90
Manchester United/City	96
Manchester United Ice Rink	96
Manto	68
Marble Beer House	33
Market Street	72
Megabowl	98
MEN Arena	95
The Metropolitan	41
Mint Lounge	58
Mojo	35
Mr Thomas's Chop House	39
The Music Box	59

N

National Express	120
New Union	68
Night & Day Café	47

O

O'Neills	40
Odd	47
The Odeon at The Filmworks	88
Ohm	59
Oi Polloi	74
Oklahoma	11
The Old Grapes	39
The Old House at Home	52
The Old Nags Head	39
The Old Wellington Inn	37
Olive Delicatessen	11 & 66
The Olive Press	21
Olivier Morosini	116
One Central Street	59
One Night Stand	89
The Orange Grove	45
The Ox Hotel	31
Oxfam Bookshop	79
Oxfam Originals	78

P

The Palace Theatre and The Opera House	93
Panacea Bar & Restaurant	38
Paparazzi	60
The Phoenix	60
Piccadilly Bus Station	120
Piccadilly Records	80
Pitcher and Piano	40
Po Na Na	61
Pop Boutique	75
Premier Travel Inn	111
Princess Hotel	110
Pumpkins	75

Q

The Queen of Hearts	61

R

Rags 2 Bitches	76
The Rampant Lion	51
Ran	77
Reiss	76
Rhubarb	22
The Roadhouse	61
Robinskis	45
Royal Exchange Theatre	93
Royal Orchid	22

S

Sandbar	50
Sankey's	62
Satan's Hollow	62
Sawyers Arms	39
Schuh	77
Selfridges in the City	73
Shiva Body Piercing	116
Siam Orchid	23

www.itchymanchester.co.uk

Index

Sir Ralph Abercrombie	37
The Slug & Lettuce	40
Snook	43
Sola	50
South	62
St Ann's Hospice Furniture Shop	78
Stanfords	79
The Station	41
Stay Inn	111
System One Travelcards	95 & 118

T

Tampopo	23
Taurus	66
Teppanyaki	23
The Thirsty Scholar	51
Thunder Egg	84
The Titchy Coffee Company	11
Toni and Guy Academy	116
Trafford Centre	100
Travelling Man	84
Travelodge	111
The Triangle	73
Tribeca	35
Trof	43
Try Thai	24

U

Umami	24
Urban Outfitters	75
Urulu	32

V

Velvet	67
Via Fossa	68
Victoria & Albert Hotel	110
Vinyl Exchange	80
Virgin Megastore	80

W

WH Smith	79
Wagamama	25
Walkabout Hotel	111
Waterstones	79
Westworld	75
The White Lion	31
The Whitworth	91
The Wilmslow Hotel	111

Y

The Y Club	117
Yang Sing	25

Z

Zen Zero	25

Itchy

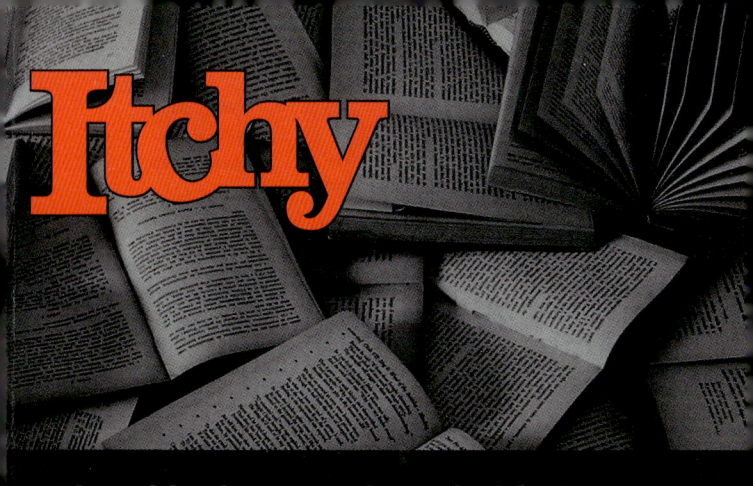

'The tables here are cleaned with the same amount of care that a dog takes wiping its arse.' *Itchy's review of a scummy bar, 2006*

'What?' You're thinking. 'You can't say that...' Oh yes we can. As the most straight talking-est, no-bullshit guide to going out in the UK, we'll never shy away from telling you if somewhere sucks harder than a toothless granny eating a boiled sweet. We also say nice things too.

www.itchycity.co.uk

Gazing at the stars

THERE'S NOTHING LIKE A GOOD CELEB SPOT TO MAKE YOUR DAY SEEM MORE EXCITING, SO HERE'S A RUNDOWN OF WHO YOU'RE LIKELY TO SEE IN MANCHESTER

Manchester has a history of being a funny city (although you wouldn't know it from some of the puns we've resuscitated from **Jasper Carrot's** joke book). Famed comedians from **Caroline Aherne** to **Eric Sykes** and **Eric Morecambe** all grew up in this part of the world, while **Steve Coogan** is often seen around town, presumably following scallies around for inspiration.

But we're not just a city of jokers and wisecrackers. Some very respectable journalists have originated from these very parts. **Anna Ford** and um... well, actually that's about it. But **Bill Oddie, Melanie Sykes, Phillip Schofield** and king of cool, **David 'what a bobby dazzler' Dickinson** also started out around here. Away from people famed for being orange, Christopher 'my nose is perfectly normal' Eccleston, Sir Ben Kingsley and Sir Ian McKellen are all Manchester-born lads. You can also catch Manchester boy **Dominic Monaghan** (one of the small folk from *Lord of the Rings*) on the sci-fi yarn, *Lost*. We can't blame him for wanting to live on a desert island – it rains less. And it probably beats solving mysteries with Hetty Wainthrop too.